D0824718

BIG RANCH, BIG CITY COOKBOOK

DOWNTOWN
LAMBERTS
BARBECUE

BIG RANCH, BIG CITY COOKBOOK

Recipes from LAMBERT'S TEXAS KITCHENS

Louis Lambert
WITH June Naylor

Photography by RALPH LAUER | Foreword by ROBB WALSH

TEN SPEED PRESS
Berkeley

To all the strong women in my life—Joann, Liz, Lucille, and Norma

Acknowledgments

THE PROCESS OF WRITING affords you the chance to sit at your computer and think about what is important. For me, more than anything, it's the people in my life who I value and who have made this book possible.

June Naylor, my good friend and coauthor, is the reason this book was written. Thank you for believing in me and leading me by the hand through this journey.

I'm so thankful for Lisa Ekus, my agent, and her team for the behind the scenes work they have done in helping to create this book. I still owe all of you a trip to West Texas.

Thanks to all the folks at Ten Speed, especially Melissa Moore, who paved the way for me with such a warm welcome, designer Toni Tajima for a gorgeous layout, and our editor Veronica Randall, for sharing my vision and enthusiasm for the concept and feel of *Big Ranch, Big City*.

Ralph Lauer, our photographer, captured the majestic beauty of Texas and the simple and approachable feel of the foods that I love to cook and eat. Thank you Ralph.

Thanks to Cynthia Wahl and Media Kessler for your hard work, insight, and friendship.

Thank you Larry McGuire and Tommy Morman, the guys who operate Lambert's in Austin, for your style and spot on sensibility. I'm proud of you guys for the food you cook and the restaurants that you create and run.

Nate Watson, thanks for your friendship and hard work in testing recipes. The rest of the boys in the dinner club, Bill, Jace, and Joel, thanks for your appetites, opinions, and good humor.

All the McKnight cousins, especially Bob, thank you for putting up with all of us at the ranch during the production of this book.

Mom, thanks for always listening and giving me a shoulder. Dad, thanks for giving me an enthusiasm for food and the ability to tell a story. Liz, thanks for being the person I can call on for advice and council. James, thanks for standing by me and keeping me pointed in the right direction.

Contents

SALADS

SOUPS & STEWS

SAUSAGES, PÂTÉS & CURED MEATS

BEEF, LAMB, PORK & GAME

POULTRY

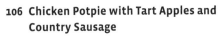

SEAFOOD

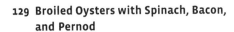

TEX-MEX

VEGETABLES & SIDES

BREADS

DESSERTS

STOCKS & SAUCES

Foreword BY ROBB WALSH

THE PHOTO OF LOUIS LAMBERT leaning on a wall that appeared in *Martha Stewart Living* in 1996 first brought him to my attention. I had to wonder: How did this young grad from The Culinary Institute of America who worked for, among others, Wolfgang Puck, end up cooking at Reata in Fort Worth and hanging out with Martha Stewart in Marfa, Texas?

I was even more intrigued by the food I saw in the article. Double-cut rib eye steaks with chimmichurri sauce, grilled red potato salad with warm bacon vinaigrette, brined corn on the cob—this stuff was nothing like the Southwestern cuisine that was in vogue at the time.

Every other chef on the scene in the mid-1990s had a label. There were "Southwestern Cuisine" chefs and "Cowboy Cuisine" chefs and "New Texas Cuisine" chefs. Louis Lambert stuck out because he seemed to be a chef without a schtick.

I got to know Lambert better by cooking his recipes. I loved his Shiner Bock-beer battered Texas 1015 onion rings, I still make his spicy bread and butter pickles, and I thank him often for his onion jam.

Today Louis Lambert has a bunch of his own restaurants in Austin and Fort Worth, and they continue to reflect his simple and direct approach to Texas cooking. There's a barbecue joint, a steakhouse, a hamburger stand, and a couple of coffee shops. An idea he's kicking around now is a coffee and fried pie trailer. The food at all of Louis Lambert's restaurants is amazingly tasty. It also manages to be both unpretentious and sophisticated, which is a tough thing to pull off.

In the last couple of years, I have gotten to know Louis Lambert personally as we worked together with scores of other Texas food lovers, including his coauthor, June Naylor, to create a nonprofit called Foodways Texas. And I have admired his passion for the mission of the new organization—to preserve, promote, and celebrate the diverse food cultures of Texas. His knowledge of Texas food history and culture is remarkable.

Lambert's cooking never did get saddled with a label. I was curious how he would describe it. Some of the recipes in the book come from the ranch houses and cowboy camps of the

McKnight Ranch in West Texas where he grew up and some come from his restaurants. Like most West Texas cattle folks, he is uncomfortable with any kind of praise or aggrandizement.

Personally I might describe the wonderful recipes in this book as "exciting, yet straightforward fare from a seventh-generation West Texas cattle rancher who graduated from the CIA in Hyde Park and cooked in New York and California before returning to Texas," but that's probably too long to fit on the cover.

If I had to come up with a shorter label for Louis Lambert's exceptional Texas cooking, I think I would call it, the "Aw, Shucks Cuisine."

—ROBB WALSH

Introduction

IT HAS ALWAYS BEEN INTERESTING TO ME to try and figure out how chefs develop their culinary style and why they choose to cook the foods they serve—what motivates and inspires them. As a working chef, I know I have developed a distinctive style—there are certain ingredients I love to work with, techniques and methods I am drawn to, and flavor profiles and presentations I am most comfortable with. In the business, it's known as a chef's repertoire—the foods we love to cook and the dishes our customers associate with us. Home cooks also develop their own style and repertoire. My mother's culinary repertoire was a selection of about six casseroles and three restaurants. I still make her version of Hungarian Beef Goulash—even though there's really nothing all that Hungarian about it.

The chefs and cooks that I have always had the most respect for have one thing in common—the foods they cook have a depth of soul and flavor rooted in their life experiences. My father's mother is a decedent of the original French Arcadians who settled in Louisiana. Whenever we visited Grandmom in Port Arthur, she spent all day in the kitchen making the foods my father grew up eating—stuffed deviled crab, Cajun smothered pork chops, and our favorite, shrimp gumbo, to name just a few. My earliest memory of eating barbeque was my father taking my brothers and me to Leroy's Pit Barbeque in Odessa when we were kids. Leroy, like all the old timers, made everything he served from scratch—creamy cole slaw, tangy vinegar barbecue sauce, and plump spicy hot links. My grandmother's shrimp gumbo and Leroy's hot links are examples of foods that have such a deep and unique flavor and feel eating them comes close to being a religious experience for me. There is nothing fancy about either dish, but I'd choose them over a $200 dinner in most fancy restaurants.

My mother's family has ranched in Texas for seven generations. I was raised in the West Texas town of Odessa, known for oil, ranching, and high school football when I was a kid. The closest big cities were El Paso and Fort Worth, each about a five-hour drive away. Growing up in the 1970s, there wasn't a large variety to choose from at the grocers. Beef was king and iceberg was about it for lettuce. Grilling and smoking were the preferred cooking methods, and any discussions focused on what kind of wood to use, which dry rub was best for certain cuts of meat, whether to slow-cook or cook with a hot fire, whether to mop your brisket or not, whether to go with a sweet sauce or vinegar pepper sauce, and how to convert used oil field equipment into a grill and smoker. Holiday gatherings usually involved butchering and barbecuing a *cabrito* (baby goat). If the holiday had a religious tone to it, my father would roast a big leg of lamb.

During the fall and winter months, we spent evenings and weekends at the ranch hunting dove, quail, duck, and deer. My mother, the casserole queen, stopped trying to cook game by the time I was in junior high, leaving my brothers and me to serve up what we shot. During the spring and summer there were two big cattle roundups every year and my Uncle Robert would hire a camp cook, Lilo, who prepared three meals a day over an open fire for all the cowboys: big Dutch ovens were filled with sourdough bread and sweet cobblers; breakfast meant fried eggs, buttermilk biscuits, and hot coffee; other meals were always beef, usually grilled over an open fire with loads of chiles and spice. These were the meals of my youth—big, burly foods with deep flavors and rich textures. And when broken down into their components, foods that are pretty simple and straightforward, but unrepentantly from West Texas.

Today, my cousin Bob is the only one of eleven grandkids who wanted to stay on at the ranch. Meanwhile, I went into the chef business. After earning a bachelor's degree in hotel-restaurant management and graduating from The Culinary Institute of America, I took cooking jobs in New York, Dallas, and San Francisco—the chef's journey of paying his dues in big-name restaurants in big-name cities. Part of that journey is about figuring out who you are, what you want to cook, and how you want to cook it. It's about discovering what will keep you passionate and excited about food twelve hours a day, seven days a week.

My awakening came when I was working at Wolfgang Puck's Postrio in San Francisco. I was working the different positions in the kitchen when I was given the chance to work in the butcher and charcuterie shop. There we butchered whole chickens, ducks, lambs, and fish into center-of-the-palate portions, taking the trim and tuning it into sausages, rillettes, and ballontines. All the hams, pastramis, smoked salmon, and sturgeon were cured and smoked in-house. Of course, all the techniques and recipes were old-school European, but to me they were straight out of my childhood, just citified and fancied up.

In San Francisco, we made duck sausage with dried fruit and pistachios. In Odessa, we made venison hotlinks with jalapeño and cheddar. Same technique, just different ingredients. At Postrio, I made a dish of maple sugar-cured and grilled Wolf Farms quail with wild blackberry compote. But it was just an urban rendition of an old West Texas standard that used brown sugar, chili powder, and small fryer chickens. It was then that I realized that I could cook the foods that I grew up with and loved while using the techniques and methods I had learned at CIA and big city restaurants.

When I moved back to Texas for good, in 1999 my sister and I opened Jo's in Austin, an open-air coffee and sandwich shop. We made the decision to serve the foods we had a family connection to—fried pies, kolaches, and sloppy slow-smoked pulled pork sandwiches—which are still the mainstays of Jo's menu today. In 2001, I opened the first Lambert's on South Congress in Austin. A small neighborhood bistro-style restaurant. Even though we were a white-table-cloth restaurant serving steak, lamb, and seafood, we also offered chile con queso and venison pâté for appetizers, macaroni and cheese as a side dish, and maple bread pudding for dessert.

In 2006, I had the chance to partner with Larry McGuire, Tommy Morman, and Will Bridges and open Lambert's Downtown Barbecue. I credit Larry with being the vision behind the restaurant and Tommy with steering the quality of the food that comes out of the kitchen. Lambert's Downtown was built around the same philosophy of cooking—jalapeño cheddar hotlinks, smoked beef brisket, maple sugar and mustard crusted rib eye steaks, and crispy wild boar ribs—all foods we grew up eating, we just enhance the flavors with the best ingredients possible and proper cooking techniques.

Lambert's Steaks and Seafood in Fort Worth was inspired by old-school Texas steak houses. The menu offers grilled quail, prime rib of beef, wood grilled steaks, fresh gulf seafood, and chicken fried steak with cream gravy. And for dessert, you can try to resist the buttermilk chocolate cake, the rich Mexican flan, the sweet peach cake cobbler, or Lambert's fudge brownie with a big scoop of chocolate mocha ice cream.

In writing this cookbook, I've tried to take the same approach that I do when creating menus at my restaurants—I'm sharing my West Texas heritage by putting it right on the plate, with some urban updates. A recent restaurant review said of my food, *"This is food that your grandparents might have served, if your grandparents had either had some formal culinary train- ing, or had been seriously addicted to the Food Network"*. I take this as a compliment. I think that like my grandmother and Leroy, my food is a reflection of the place and people I came from and my love and respect of what it means to be a chef.

SALADS

WHEN I WAS A KID IN ODESSA, our choices for lettuce in the grocery store were limited to iceberg and green leaf, so the typical green salad usually just had chopped iceberg with a little tomato and cucumber. That's probably why rural folks are still pretty good at turning almost anything into a salad: potato salad, three-bean salad, pasta salad, and coleslaw are pretty much the mainstays at potluck suppers where I come from. My grandmother was very fond of congealed fruit salad, and her standard was made with canned fruit enclosed within some type of green gelatin that had been turned to a soft opaque shade with a little mayonnaise and was presented on iceberg lettuce leaves. She would trot out her fruit salad when it was her turn to host the Odessa Bridge Club or for festive holiday dinners with the family. I'll even admit that I'm still fond of a salad made of cubed cheddar cheese, peas, and pimentos, all bound together with a little mayonnaise. It's a good thing that we've come a long way with salads today. Thanks to modern grocery stores, even folks out in West Texas can buy micro greens, teardrop tomatoes, and fresh herbs.

The foundation of all green salads is the lettuce, which will determine the texture and base flavor of the finished plate. Many salads are built around one type of green, such as crisp, sweet romaine in a Caesar salad, or a soft, earthy spinach in a warm spinach salad. Other salads use greens to balance out other ingredients: the watercress in the red grapefruit and avocado salad gives the dish a crisp texture and a little heat to balance out the sweet acid of the grapefruit and the fat of the avocado. A simple mixed green salad can be a perfect place to begin a meal. Unfortunately, most cafés and restaurants today use a premixed bag of nondescript, limp "baby" greens that lack flavor and texture. You are much better off selecting two or three seasonal greens that work together. The Italian *tricolore* salad, for example, is a perfectly simple combination of radicchio, endive, and arugula dressed with balsamic vinegar and shavings of Parmesan. My theory is that an uncomplicated salad is always the best.

Other ingredients that can be added to a salad are almost endless: toasted and spiced nuts, cheeses, croutons, herbs, fruits, vegetables, and meats. Again, it is best to keep salads fairly simple and limit the number of ingredients. More is not always better. All the elements of a salad must serve the purpose of adding to the taste or texture of the finished dish. Don't be tempted to add nonfunctional garnishes or ingredients that only look good.

The one thing all salads have in common, whether they're made from greens, potatoes, or some other ingredient, is that they have some type of dressing. Dressing a salad can be as simple as squeezing lemon juice and sprinkling good olive oil on tender young greens, or it can be a bit more complex, like preparing a rémoulade using homemade mayonnaise for poached shrimp and crab. In its simplest form, a dressing is an acid combined with a fat. The acid in a dressing can be juice from a citrus fruit, such as lemons, limes, oranges, and grapefruit, or it can be a vinegar, such as apple cider, wine, sherry, or balsamic vinegar, to name just a few. Keep in mind that the different citrus juices and vinegars have different levels of acidity, which will change the flavor of your finished vinaigrette. I like to combine different citrus juices and vinegars to help balance the flavors and acid levels in vinaigrettes, using sherry vinegar and lemon juice together, for example, or combining white wine vinegar with a splash of balsamic.

Cooks today also have a lot of fats to choose from: vegetable oils, olive oil, nut oils, dairy creams, and animal fats like bacon drippings. Again, don't be afraid to mix different oils in a dressing to balance the flavor of the finished dish. Many oils and fats are too bold on their own and should only be used to finish or flavor a dressing. I will often make a basic vinaigrette with a neutral-flavored vegetable oil and finish it with an expensive and flavorful olive oil. On its own, a bold olive oil will often overpower everything else in a salad. All the ingredients in a salad should complement each other, and a balanced dressing should tie all the ingredients together.

When you are ready to assemble and dress your salad, make sure all the ingredients are dry. Whether you are working with greens, potatoes, beets, or beans, moisture will not only keep your dressing from adhering to the ingredients, but it will also result in a watery salad. Before you dress your salad, taste the dressing by dipping a leaf into it. This is the best way to tell if you need to adjust the seasoning. Use a mixing bowl that is much larger than the volume of salad you are preparing to give yourself plenty of room to toss and mix. Drizzle the dressing evenly over the top of the salad before tossing. If you overdress a salad, the dressing will weigh down the greens and it will be all you can taste. Tender greens with a delicate flavor need to be lightly dressed and gently tossed. Bolder greens and sturdier vegetables can stand up to more and heavier dressings. In either case, the best tool for mixing a salad is your hands. Your hands are perfectly made to gently lift and work the dressing into the salad. I usually add any additional ingredients or garnishes, such as nuts, cheese, or herbs, to the salad after I have dressed the greens. This is so the dressing won't mask the appearance and flavor of the extra ingredients. Use the following recipes as a guide and inspiration in creating your own repertoire of salads.

Beef Salpicon Salad

My father used to take my brothers and me hunting for whitetail deer at our ranch in Carrizo Springs, in southwest Texas near the Mexican border. After a long day of hunting, we would cross the Rio Grande for dinner at the Moderno in Piedras Negras, Mexico. It's one of those classic border restaurants, with professional waiters in white jackets and a roaming mariachi band. It was at the Moderno that I was first turned on to beef salpicon. I had eaten plenty of brisket in my life, but nothing as complex as a fatty brisket slow-cooked with chiles, onion, and garlic. Beef salpicon salad has become a mainstay on our menu. This beef also makes great stuffing for enchiladas and chiles rellenos.

MAKES 6 TO 8 SERVINGS

BRISKET

3 pounds flat-cut beef brisket, excess fat trimmed

3 ancho chiles, stemmed and seeded

1 yellow onion, coarsely chopped

3 cloves garlic, coarsely chopped

2 plum tomatoes, cored and coarsely chopped

2 teaspoons dried oregano

1 bay leaf

2 teaspoons kosher salt

1 teaspoon freshly ground black pepper

SALAD

2 heads romaine lettuce

5 radishes, thinly sliced

1/2 small red onion, thinly sliced

Juice of 2 limes

3 tablespoons olive oil

1 tablespoon honey

Salt

2 firm, ripe avocados

2 poblano chiles, roasted, and cut into strips

1/2 cup chopped cilantro

4 ounces queso fresco, crumbled

24 corn tortillas, warmed

Place the brisket, chiles, onion, garlic, tomatoes, oregano, bay leaf, salt, and pepper in a pot with enough water to cover. Bring to a simmer, cover, and slowly cook the brisket until it is fork-tender and beginning to fall apart, about 3 1/2 hours. Let the brisket cool at room temperature in the cooking liquid for about 30 minutes.

Transfer the brisket to a work surface and, using two forks, shred the brisket into small pieces. Put the shredded brisket into a large mixing bowl.

Discard the bay leaf from the cooking liquid and, using a slotted spoon, scoop out all of the solids—chiles, onions, tomatoes, and garlic—and put into a blender. Add 2 cups of the cooking liquid to the solids and puree until smooth. Add the puree to the shredded brisket and stir to coat the meat. Taste for salt and pepper and adjust the seasoning, if needed.

To make the salad, split the heads of romaine lengthwise down the center and then cut across into 1-inch strips. Wash and dry the lettuce and put in a large mixing bowl with the radishes and red onion. Next, whisk together the lime juice, olive oil, and honey with a pinch of salt in a small bowl. Pour the dressing over the lettuce and toss to combine.

Line a large platter with the dressed salad. Mound the brisket on top of the lettuce and garnish with the avocado, roasted poblanos, cilantro, and queso fresco. Serve with plenty of warm griddled corn tortillas.

Lambert's Chopped Salad

This is a variation on a salad that was served at Mac's House Restaurant in Fort Worth, where I would eat with my parents when we were in town to watch a Texas Christian University football game. Mac's House is no longer in business, so when I moved to Fort Worth I came up with my version of that great dish and put it on the menu as our house salad. I think you'll find it's a perfect way to start any meal.

MAKES 6 SERVINGS

3 tablespoons fresh lemon juice

3 tablespoons white wine vinegar

¼ cup honey

¼ cup canola oil

1 large clove garlic, minced

Salt and freshly ground black pepper

4 cups iceberg lettuce, chopped into 3-inch pieces

4 cups romaine lettuce, chopped into 3-inch pieces

¼ cup finely diced green onions, white and green parts

3 tablespoons sesame seeds (white and black), toasted

½ cup sliced almonds, toasted

½ cup freshly grated Parmesan cheese

To make the dressing, combine the lemon juice, vinegar, honey, canola oil, and garlic in a small mixing bowl and whisk to combine. Season with salt and pepper and store in the refrigerator until ready to assemble the salad.

To assemble the salad, combine the lettuces and green onions in a large serving bowl and add enough dressing to coat. Add the sesame seeds, almonds, and Parmesan and lightly toss. Serve the salad immediately.

Ranch Steak Salad Niçoise

I originally came up with this salad when I had a leftover grilled steak in the refrigerator and wanted something light for lunch. I loved the way that all the flavors worked together, so I fancied it up a bit and put it on our lunch menu. What's not to love? You have steak, potatoes, green beans, and a salad all on one plate.

MAKES 4 SERVINGS

STEAK AND POTATOES

2 (12-ounce) strip steaks, each about 1¹/₂ inches thick

Olive oil, for drizzling and for the pan

Kosher salt and freshly ground black pepper

1 tablespoon coarsely chopped fresh thyme

12 small new potatoes, cooked in boiling water until fork-tender, and halved

SALAD

2 small cloves garlic, minced

1 teaspoon Dijon mustard

2 tablespoons peach jam

¹/₄ cup white wine vinegar

¹/₄ cup olive oil

Kosher salt and freshly ground black pepper

2 heads Bibb lettuce, coarsely torn

4 ounces haricots verts (French green beans), trimmed and blanched

3 plum tomatoes, cored and coarsely chopped

¹/₂ small red onion, thinly sliced

12 kalamata olives, halved

2 tablespoons finely chopped chives

2 tablespoons coarsely chopped flat-leaf parsley

2 hard-boiled eggs, quartered

Preheat your oven to 375°F. Lightly drizzle each side of both steaks with a little olive oil. Season both sides with salt and pepper and sprinkle with the thyme.

Heat a large sauté pan over high heat and then coat the bottom of the pan with olive oil. Add the steaks to the pan and cook the first side until a crisp dark-brown crust develops, about 3 minutes. Turn the steaks and cook the second side until they are browned and crusty as well. Flip the steaks again and place the sauté pan in the oven for the steaks to finish cooking, about 5 minutes for medium rare. Remove the steaks from the oven and transfer to a plate to rest while you finish the salad.

Remove all but about 2 tablespoons of oil from the sauté pan the steaks were cooked in and return the pan to the stove over medium-high heat. Add the halved potatoes to the pan in a single layer, cut side down, and lightly season with salt and pepper. Allow the potatoes to begin to brown slightly before you stir them. Continue to cook the potatoes until they are lightly seared and warmed through. Transfer the potatoes from the pan to a warm plate.

To make the dressing, in a small bowl, combine the garlic, mustard, peach jam, vinegar, and olive oil. Add a pinch of salt and pepper and whisk until the dressing comes together.

In a large mixing bowl, combine the Bibb lettuce, haricots verts, tomatoes, onions, and olives. Trim any excess fat from the steaks and cut into thin slices. Add the steak, potatoes, and half of the chives and parsley to the salad bowl and toss with enough of the dressing to lightly coat. Divide the salad between 4 plates, garnish with the egg quarters, and sprinkle with the remaining chives and parsley. Serve immediately.

Red Grapefruit and Avocado Salad with Honey-Poppy Seed Dressing

My West Texas grandmother, Lucille, served a grapefruit and avocado salad whenever she hosted the Odessa Bridge Club. Today we serve a jazzed-up version of Lucille's salad at the Lambert's Restaurant, adding watercress and pine nuts for crunch and goat cheese for a bit of tang.

MAKES 6 SERVINGS

2 tablespoons honey, preferably Tupelo

2 tablespoons fresh lime juice

1 tablespoon red wine vinegar

1 tablespoon vegetable oil

2 tablespoons sour cream

1 teaspoon poppy seeds

Salt and freshly ground black pepper

3 tablespoons pine nuts

3 red grapefruit

2 Hass avocados, cut into 1-inch dice

2 ounces fresh goat cheese, crumbled

2 bunches of watercress, thick stems removed

1 tablespoon minced chives

In a small bowl, whisk the honey with the lime juice, vinegar, oil, and sour cream. Stir in the poppy seeds and season with salt and pepper.

In a small skillet, toast the pine nuts over medium heat, shaking the pan, until golden brown, about 2 minutes.

Using a sharp knife, peel the grapefruit, being sure to remove all of the bitter white pith. Working over a large bowl, cut in between the membranes to release the sections. Reserve the grapefruit juice for another use. Pat the grapefruit sections dry with paper towels and put them in the serving bowl.

Add the avocado, goat cheese, and watercress to the bowl and toss gently. Add the chives, pine nuts, and the dressing and toss again. Serve immediately.

[Red Grapefruit]

The Lower Rio Grande Valley in south Texas is one of the leading producers of red grapefruit in America. Florida may produce more grapefruit, but nothing compares to a south Texas red grapefruit for its deep color and perfect balance of sweetness. Named for the grapelike clusters in which it grows, grapefruit was first introduced to south Texas in the 1890s. Early farmers recognized that the valley's fertile soil, sunny weather, and tropical climate were perfectly suited for citrus production. Today, Texas red grapefruit are marketed under two names, Ruby-Sweet and the Rio Star.

When buying grapefruit, pick fruit that feel heavy for their size, since heavy fruit contain lots of juice. Don't be afraid of fruit with blemishes; they don't affect the fruit inside. These blemishes, which farmers call "tropical beauty marks," are caused by the breezes rubbing the fruit in the trees. Grapefruit can be stored in a cool area for up to 2 weeks and are fine the refrigerator for up to 6 weeks.

Fried Green Tomatoes with Crab Rémoulade

Dean Ridge, one of our neighbors in Odessa, loved to grow tomatoes. Early in the summer, his wife, Barbara, would pick some of the green ones and fry them up in a cornmeal batter. I loved the tartness of the green tomatoes encased in a crisp cornmeal crust, so I would always try to get invited to eat dinner with them when I knew Barbara was making them. When I started cooking for a living, I remembered Barbara's tomatoes and started serving them with a sweet crab salad with a Creole rémoulade and a rich tomato vinaigrette.

MAKES 6 SERVINGS

4 cups vegetable oil

2 eggs

1/4 cup milk

1 1/4 cups all-purpose flour

2 cups cornmeal

4 to 5 green tomatoes, cored and sliced 1/4-inch thick

Kosher salt and finely ground black pepper

Crab Rémoulade

Tomato Vinaigrette (page 20), for drizzling

Heat a large skillet with the vegetable oil over medium-high heat until the oil reaches 375°F. Whisk together the eggs and milk in a small mixing bowl. In a separate bowl, combine 1 cup of the flour and cornmeal, season with salt and pepper, and transfer to a large plate.

To fry the tomatoes, dust both sides with the remaining flour, lightly dip in the egg mixture, and then coat both sides with the cornmeal mixture. Carefully drop in the hot oil and fry each side for about 2 minutes, or until golden brown. Transfer the fried tomatoes to a plate lined with paper towels and hold in a low oven to keep warm while you finish frying all the tomatoes.

To serve, top each tomato with a spoonful of the Crab Rémoulade and a drizzle of Tomato Vinaigrette.

CRAB RÉMOULADE

MAKES 6 SERVINGS

1 pound lump fresh crabmeat, picked over for bits of shell

1 shallot, finely diced

2 tablespoons finely diced celery

2 green onions, white and green parts, finely diced

2 tablespoons flat-leaf parsley, finely chopped

3/4 cup mayonnaise

2 tablespoons Dijon mustard

2 tablespoons ketchup

1 tablespoon prepared horseradish

1/2 teaspoon Worcestershire sauce

1 teaspoon Tabasco sauce

Kosher salt and finely ground black pepper

2 teaspoons paprika

Stir together all the ingredients in mixing bowl until well combined. Store in a covered container in the refrigerator.

(continued on next page)

(Fried Green Tomatoes with Crab Rémoulade, continued)

TOMATO VINAIGRETTE

MAKES 1 CUP

½ cup olive oil

1 clove garlic, crushed then coarsely chopped

3 ripe plum tomatoes, cored, seeded, and cut into ½-inch dice

Kosher salt and freshly ground black pepper

1 tablespoon tomato paste

½ teaspoon sugar

¼ cup white wine vinegar

Heat the olive oil in a medium saucepan over medium-high heat. Add the garlic and tomatoes and cook until the tomatoes begin to break down, about 3 minutes. Season with salt and pepper and stir in the tomato paste and sugar.

Remove the saucepan from the heat and allow to cool for about 5 minutes. Stir in the vinegar and then process the vinaigrette through a food mill into a small bowl. Taste and adjust the seasoning, if needed. (If you don't have a food mill, it's okay to pulse in a food processor until finely chopped.)

[Vinaigrette]

In its most basic form, a vinaigrette is a combination of three parts oil to one part vinegar. Of course, vinaigrettes are usually used to dress salads, but we also use them as marinades and as light sauces for vegetables, meat, and fish. A vinaigrette can be as simple as stirring together some olive oil with your favorite vinegar, or it can be a thick and creamy Caesar dressing emulsified with egg yolks, mustard, and Parmesan cheese.

Please allow me to give you a nonscientific cook's perspective on emulsions and vinaigrettes. An emulsion is formed when two or more usually unblendable liquids—oil and vinegar, for example—are joined into one liquid using physical and chemical forces. To make an emulsified vinaigrette, you start with the vinegar in a mixing bowl and gradually add the oil in a steady stream while whisking vigorously. The fat molecules are being broken apart by the whisking motion, which allows the fat to surround the vinegar molecules. We have all seen, though, how our vinaigrettes will eventually separate again into layers of oil and vinegar. To stabilize the emulsion, we can increase the physical force and add emulsifiers. Physically, you can whisk your dressing like a madman as you add the oil to the vinegar, scaring the dog and your kids, or you can just make the vinaigrette in a blender to strengthen the emulsion. My mother used to make a vinaigrette by wildly shaking a glass jar over her head. Adding emulsifiers like egg yolks, mustard, and honey not only help in forming and thickening the vinaigrette, but they also help to stabilize the emulsion once it is made. Don't tell anybody, but when I'm throwing together a creamy vinaigrette at the house for friends, I'll quickly whisk together a little olive oil, garlic, lemon juice, salt, and pepper and then add a big dollop of mayonnaise to bring the whole thing together. It makes the perfect tart and creamy vinaigrette, so thoroughly emulsified that you could drive it to New York and back and it still wouldn't separate.

Warm German Potato Salad

Any kind of creamer potato, like Yukon Gold, works well in this recipe, but I like to use Red Bliss potatoes. When I'm serving this dish with barbecue or taking it to an informal potluck, I don't bother peeling the potatoes. When I'm trying to be fancy, I'll peel the potatoes after they are cooked.

MAKES 8 SERVINGS

3 pounds Red Bliss or other creamer potatoes

1/2 pound bacon

1 large yellow onion, diced medium

3/4 cup cider vinegar

1/4 cup sugar

1 tablespoon Dijon mustard

2 tablespoons vegetable oil

Kosher salt and freshly ground black pepper

8 green onions, green and white parts, thinly sliced

1/2 cup chopped flat-leaf parsley

Cover the potatoes with cold water in a large pot, bring to a simmer, and cook until just fork-tender, about 15 minutes. Drain the potatoes in a colander and let cool until they are cool enough to handle. Cut the potatoes into 1/4-inch slices and place in a large covered bowl to keep warm.

In a large sauté pan over medium-high heat, cook the bacon until it is crisp. Transfer the bacon from the pan to your cutting board and chop. Set aside on a plate. Return the sauté pan with the rendered bacon fat to the stove over medium-high heat. Add the onion and cook until soft and beginning to brown, about 4 minutes. Carefully stir in the vinegar, sugar, mustard, and vegetable oil. Season with salt and pepper and bring the dressing to a simmer. Pour the hot dressing over the warm potatoes and fold in the bacon, green onions, and parsley. Serve immediately, or at room temperature.

Roasted Beet Salad with Shaved Fennel and Candied Shallot Vinaigrette

Beets have always been one of my favorite root vegetables, and roasting them helps bring out the vegetable's sweet, earthy flavor that I love so much. It's also one of the easiest ways to cook a beet. After the beets are roasted, the skins will usually peel off very easily; I usually use kitchen gloves or an old kitchen towel. Crisp licorice-like fennel, tart goat cheese, and rich toasted walnuts add layers of texture and flavor to the roasted beets. The final punch in this salad is a dressing made by candying shallots in orange juice and sugar. Even if you are one of those unfortunate souls that doesn't like beets, please try the Candied Shallot Vinaigrette on your other salads.

MAKES 6 SERVINGS

2¹/₂ pounds small to medium beets

2 tablespoons olive oil

1 cup Candied Shallot Vinaigrette (page 24)

1 small fennel bulb

1 head Bibb lettuce

Salt and freshly ground black pepper

¹/₂ cup crumbled fresh goat cheese

¹/₄ cup walnut pieces, toasted

Preheat your oven to 350°F.

Trim the tops off the beets and lightly scrub under running water. Dry the beets and lightly coat with the olive oil. Place the beets on a baking sheet and roast in the oven until tender and a knife blade can be easily inserted into the center, about 45 minutes. Allow the beets to cool, peel, and then cut into bite-sized pieces. Place the beets in a bowl and lightly coat with ¹/₂ cup of the vinaigrette. Cover, and place in the refrigerator to cool.

With a sharp chef's knife, trim the fronds off the fennel bulb and then trim the root end, being careful to leave enough of the bottom to continue holding the bulb together. Cutting from the top of the bulb to the bottom, shave the bulb into strips about ¹/₈ inch thick. Next, lay the strips flat on your cutting board and cut again into strips ¹/₈ inch wide. Transfer the fennel to a small bowl of ice water to crisp up for about 15 minutes.

To assemble the salad, use the six largest lettuce leaves to form 6 baskets. Coarsely chop the remainder of the lettuce and fill the baskets halfway with chopped lettuce. Add the shaved fennel to the beets and season with salt and black pepper. Top each lettuce basket with the beets and fennel. Lightly drizzle each basket with the remaining vinaigrette. Sprinkle the goat cheese and walnuts over each basket and serve.

(continued on next page)

(Roasted Beet Salad with Shaved Fennel and Candied Shallot Vinaigrette, continued)

CANDIED SHALLOT VINAIGRETTE

MAKES 2 CUPS

2 large shallots, medium dice

1 cup orange juice

¹/₂ cup sugar

2 teaspoons Dijon mustard

2 tablespoons fresh lemon juice

¹/₄ cup white wine vinegar

Salt and freshly ground black pepper

¹/₂ cup olive oil

1 tablespoon finely chopped chives

Combine the shallots, orange juice, and sugar in a small saucepan and bring to a simmer. Reduce the heat to low and slowly cook until the orange juice has reduced by a third, about 20 minutes. Transfer the shallots and their liquid to a blender. Add the mustard, lemon juice, vinegar, and salt and pepper to taste. Turn the blender on low and drizzle in the olive oil while the motor is running. Remove the vinaigrette from the blender and stir in the chives. (Store any remaining vinaigrette, covered, in the refrigerator for up to four days.)

Spinach Salad with Smoked Bacon Vinaigrette and Blue Cheese

This is a classic restaurant salad that goes great with anything from steak to seafood. I stole the idea of using malt vinegar in a spinach salad from my friend Grady Spears, a chef in Fort Worth. It adds just the right amount of acid as well as a nice sweetness that goes great with spinach, bacon, and blue cheese.

MAKES 4 SERVINGS

1 pound baby spinach

5 slices smoked bacon, chopped

3 tablespoons shallots, diced small

1/2 cup malt vinegar

2 tablespoons olive oil

1 teaspoon Dijon mustard

1 teaspoon sugar

Kosher salt and freshly ground black pepper

2 ounces blue cheese, crumbled

2 hard-boiled eggs, finely chopped

Wash the spinach by placing it in a sink full of cold water, gently swirling it around, and then removing the spinach to a colander, leaving the water and any dirt behind. Stem the spinach, pat dry, and transfer to a large serving bowl.

In a skillet over medium-high heat, cook the bacon until crisp and transfer to a plate lined with a paper towel. Remove all but about 2 tablespoons of the bacon fat from the pan. Chop up the bacon and set aside.

Return the pan to the stove and sauté the shallots over medium heat until they begin to soften, about 1 minute. Stir in the vinegar, olive oil, mustard, and sugar and lightly season with salt and pepper. Cook until the vinaigrette just comes to a simmer.

Allow the dressing to cool while assembling the salad. Add the dressing, bacon, and blue cheese to the spinach and toss to combine. Divide the spinach between 4 plates and sprinkle each with the chopped egg. Serve immediately.

[Blue Cheese]

Blue cheese is one of those foods that people either love or hate. I love it. In a creamy salad dressing, melted over a charred piece of beef, or stuffed in a poached pear for dessert: these are only a few of the ways I love to serve it. Blue cheese (sometimes spelled "bleu" cheese) is made from cow's, sheep's, or goat's milk that has had *Penicillium* cultures added so that the cheese is spotted or veined with blue, blue-gray, or blue-green mold. The mold is what gives the cheese its distinct sharp and salty taste and strong odor. The folks in Europe give their blue cheese fancy names like Roquefort, Gorgonzola, and Stilton, because like wine, they have a protected designation of origin and can carry that particular name only if they were made in a particular region of a certain country.

Blue cheeses can vary in the intensity of their flavor and their pungency, depending on both the cheesemaker and how long they have been aged. Blue cheese is best when allowed to come to room temperature before serving.

SOUPS & STEWS

M Y PORT ARTHUR GRANDMOTHER'S GUMBO was a big part of the reason I became a chef. When the family would visit her down on the Texas coast, I would watch her in the kitchen cooking a big pot of seafood gumbo. It was probably the first time in my life that I watched someone cook with the purpose of learning what she was doing. How did Grandmom make a roux? What went into her seasoning mix for the gumbo? When did she add the shrimp and oysters to the pot? My motivation wasn't academic but purely selfish, because my mother didn't cook gumbo and my brothers and I loved it. If we were going to eat gumbo back in Odessa, I was going to have to make it.

After watching her at the stove over the course of a few pots of gumbo, the thing that struck me was not the ingredients in the gumbo or the order she put them in the pot; I was more captivated by *how* she cooked. There was a flow to her movements, almost a choreographed ease with which she moved about the kitchen. There were no cookbooks or recipes in sight, no starting and stopping, just a calm of constant cooking. I wanted to cook like my grandmother, not only in the way she put food on the table but also with her same sense of ease and grace.

After kicking around a few kitchens and restaurants in Texas, I ended up at The Culinary Institute in Hyde Park, New York. The first kitchen class I had was Skills 1, and the first thing we learned to cook was soup: onion soup, vegetable soup, consommé, cream of mushroom soup, pea soup, and clam chowder. Each was taught for a reason, as a lesson in the proper technique and the proper ingredients for cooking the different types of soups. We learned how you correctly sweat the vegetables and add them to a properly prepared chicken stock for a proper clear soup, and how you always finish a cream soup with heated cream to avoid curdling the soup. I learned how to make all the soup and stew varieties based on classical cooking techniques. I learned what ingredients went into each soup, how to cook them, and when to put them in the pot. What the instructors didn't teach me was how to cook like my grandmother. You see, that kind of cooking only comes from years of cooking the foods that you love and that are part of your life and your heritage. That is what my grandmother's gumbo was to her, and has become to me.

All of the soups and stews in this chapter bring back memories of people, places, and events in my life. Whenever I make a big batch of West Texas Venison Chili, I think of all the great hunts I've been on and all the crazy friends I've ridden with in the back of Jeeps in the dead of winter. New Mexico Pork and Green Chile Stew takes me back to our family summer trips through Santa Fe and eating in the dining room at the Plaza Real. Cannellini Soup with Parmesan and Baby Greens takes me back to the days I cooked in San Francisco and would spend my days off in North Beach sipping coffee and eating in the neighborhood's Italian restaurants.

I was first turned on to an authentic bowl of tortilla soup at Benito's in Fort Worth after a night of partying with my brother, Lyndon, about thirty years ago. I still eat at Benito's about once a week and always get a bowl of their tortilla soup and think of my brother.

Roasted Poblano and Cheddar Soup

This is my version of a cheese soup, since I figured the only way you could improve on a rich, creamy bowl of cheese soup was to add some roasted green chiles to it. For a spicier version, add a couple of finely diced jalapeños to the onions when you are sautéing them. If you can't get poblano chiles at your market, make the soup with canned green chiles instead.

MAKES 8 SERVINGS

3 tablespoons olive oil

2 tablespoons unsalted butter

1 medium yellow onion, finely chopped

4 cloves garlic, minced

2 plum tomatoes, cored, seeded, and finely chopped

1/4 cup finely chopped cilantro

1/2 cup all-purpose flour

2 cups chicken stock

1 cup whole milk

2 cups heavy cream

1 teaspoon salt

1/2 teaspoon white pepper

1/2 teaspoon dried oregano

2 poblano chiles, roasted, peeled, seeded, and finely diced

3 cups shredded white cheddar cheese

1/2 cup shredded sharp yellow cheddar cheese, for garnish

3 green onions, white and green parts, thinly sliced, for garnish

Heat a heavy soup pot over medium heat and add the olive oil and butter. When the butter is melted, add the onion and sauté until soft, about 3 minutes. Then add the garlic, tomatoes, and cilantro and continue to cook for another 2 minutes. Add the flour and cook for 2 minutes, stirring continuously.

Whisk in the chicken stock, milk, and cream and bring the soup to a brisk simmer. Season with the salt, white pepper, and oregano. Turn the heat to a low simmer and continue to cook the soup, stirring frequently, until it is thick and creamy, about 15 minutes.

Fold the poblanos into the soup and cook for 5 minutes. Add the white cheddar and stir until the cheese is incorporated and the soup is smooth, about 2 minutes. Once the cheese has been added, keep the heat at a low simmer (too high a heat will break the cheese, causing an oily soup). Ladle the soup into warm bowls and garnish with the yellow cheddar and green onions.

Ancho Chicken Tortilla Soup

A classic first course in Mexico, tortilla soup is a very simple tomato soup seasoned with onion and chiles, with crisp corn tortilla strips added just before it is served. I have kept my tortilla soup very traditional, adding chicken and some avocado, sour cream, and cheese as a garnish. The ancho chiles—a dried poblano chile—give the soup an earthy, smoky flavor with just a hint of heat.

MAKES 8 SERVINGS

1 whole cooked chicken, 3½ to 4 pounds, roasted or poached

2 tablespoons vegetable oil

1 large yellow onion, diced small

4 cloves garlic, minced

Ancho Chile Puree

2 teaspoons kosher salt

1 teaspoon freshly ground black pepper

1 teaspoon sugar

½ teaspoon dried oregano leaves

¼ cup coarsely chopped cilantro, plus more for garnish

1 (28-ounce) can chopped tomatoes, drained

4 cups chicken stock

Juice of 1 lime

8 corn tortillas, cut into 1½-inch squares and fried, or store-bought tortilla chips

½ cup sour cream

2 ripe Hass avocados, diced large

1 cup shredded Monterey Jack cheese

Skin and bone the cooked chicken and shred the meat into bite-size pieces. Set aside.

Heat a heavy soup pot over medium-high heat and add the vegetable oil. Add the onion and sauté until it becomes soft, about 4 minutes. Add the garlic to the pot and cook for 2 minutes. Add the chile puree, salt, black pepper, sugar, oregano, and cilantro. Cook for 2 minutes, stirring constantly to avoid scorching.

Add the tomatoes and chicken stock and bring the soup to a boil. Turn the heat to low and slowly simmer the soup for 20 to 30 minutes. Taste the soup and adjust the seasoning, if needed. Add the chicken and the juice of 1 lime.

To serve, place a few tortilla chips in the bottom of each bowl. Ladle the hot soup over the tortilla chips and top with a dollop of sour cream, diced avocado, shredded cheese, and a sprinkle of cilantro.

ANCHO CHILE PUREE

MAKES 1½ CUPS

2 ancho chiles, stemmed, seeded, and coarsely chopped

1 plum tomato, coarsely chopped

½ small yellow onion, coarsely chopped

2 cloves garlic

Pinch of kosher salt and freshly ground black pepper

1 teaspoon ground cumin

1 tablespoon cider vinegar

1 cup chicken stock

Combine all the ingredients in a small saucepan and bring to a simmer. Cook at a low simmer for 2 minutes, then cover the saucepan, turn the heat off, and allow the chiles to steep for 15 minutes. Transfer the solids and liquid to a blender and puree until smooth.

Cannellini Soup with Parmesan and Baby Greens

Bean soups are a perfect first course in the cooler months and make a great light and easy dinner in the spring and summer. Cannellinis, white Italian kidney beans, pair well with garlic, Parmesan, and baby braising greens to make a rich and full-bodied soup. Because I'm a Texan, I've used a smoked ham hock instead of Italian prosciutto in the soup for even more depth. If you can't find baby braising greens in your market, substitute your favorite regular braising greens, arugula, or spinach.

MAKES 8 SERVINGS

2 cups dry cannellini beans, soaked overnight

3 tablespoons olive oil

1 medium yellow onion, diced small

6 cloves garlic, thinly sliced

2 plum tomatoes, cored and diced small

1/2 teaspoon salt

1 teaspoon freshly ground black pepper

1 teaspoon dried oregano leaves

2 teaspoons chopped fresh rosemary

4 cups chicken stock

4 cups water

1 whole smoked ham hock, or 1/2 pound smoked ham, diced small

4 cups (4 ounces) baby braising greens, such as kale, chard, beet greens, or mustard greens

1/2 cup freshly grated Parmesan cheese

Basil pesto (page 33), for garnish

Drain the cannellini beans that you have soaked overnight.

Heat a heavy soup pot over medium-high heat and add the olive oil. Add the onion to the pot and cook until soft, about 4 minutes. Add the garlic and continue cooking for another 2 minutes, until the garlic is soft but has not yet begun to brown. Add the tomatoes, salt, pepper, oregano, and rosemary and cook until the tomatoes begin to collapse, about 2 minutes.

Add the chicken stock, water, drained beans, and ham hock to the soup pot and bring to a low boil. Turn the heat down to a simmer and cook, stirring occasionally, until the beans are tender, 1 to 1 1/2 hours. As the soup cooks and the chicken stock reduces, add additional water to keep the beans covered and the mixture soupy, between 2 and 2 1/2 cups in all.

Once the beans are cooked through, remove the ham hock from the pot. Ladle about 1 cup of cooked beans with a little liquid from the pot and put into a blender or your food processor. Pulse the beans once or twice, just until they are broken down, and add them back to the pot; this will help thicken the soup and give it a great texture. With a knife, cut off the skin from the outside of the ham hock and remove the meat from the bone. Dice the meat into small pieces and return to the bean pot.

Just before you are ready to serve the soup, add the braising greens and 1/4 cup of the Parmesan. Taste the soup for seasoning and make any adjustments, if needed. Simmer the soup until the greens wilt and just become tender, about 5 minutes. Ladle the soup into warm bowls and garnish with a sprinkling of the remaining Parmesan and a drizzle of pesto.

BASIL PESTO

½ cup loosely packed
fresh basil leaves

3 cloves garlic

Juice and zest of 1 lemon

¼ cup freshly grated
Parmesan cheese

2 tablespoons pine nuts

Salt and freshly ground
black pepper

⅓ cup olive oil

Combine all of the ingredients except the olive oil in a food processor; start the machine and drizzle in the oil with the motor running. Process for about 30 seconds. The texture should be smooth. Taste to see if seasonings need adjusting.

Gingered Acorn Squash Soup

When I opened my first restaurant (it was a kitchen, not a restaurant, serving several different businesses) in Austin, I worked with a gal named Michelle Stupka, a cook's cook who could bang the pots and pans and outproduce any man I've ever worked with in a kitchen. Michelle loved to make soups (well, I assume she loved to make soups, because she was so good at it), and she made a squash soup for a dinner party one night that was outrageously great, with a deep sweet squash flavor that was perfectly balanced by a spicy fruit undertone. It took me weeks of begging before she would tell me what the secret to her soup was: ginger and pineapple. I always make this soup with the ginger, but sometimes I use a tart apple or sweet pear in place of the pineapple. When I'm trying to be fancy, I'll make some buttered brioche croutons to sprinkle on the top.

MAKES 8 SERVINGS

2 acorn squash (approximately 6 cups cooked squash), quartered and seeded

3 tablespoons unsalted butter, melted

2 tablespoons brown sugar

1/4 teaspoon ground allspice

2 tablespoons olive oil

1 small white onion, diced small

3 tablespoons finely diced fresh ginger

1/2 cup small-diced fresh or canned pineapple

1 teaspoon salt

1/4 teaspoon white pepper

4 cups chicken stock

1 cup heavy cream

1/2 cup sour cream

2 tablespoons honey

Fresh chopped tarragon, for garnish

Preheat your oven to 400°F.

Arrange the cut squash on a baking sheet and brush the cut sides with the melted butter. Season each piece by sprinkling on the brown sugar and allspice. Bake the squash until the flesh is tender, about 30 minutes. When the squash has cooled enough to handle, scoop out the flesh and set aside.

Heat a heavy soup pot over medium-high heat and add the olive oil. Add the onion and ginger to the pot and cook until the onion becomes soft, about 4 minutes. Add the pineapple, salt, and white pepper and cook for another 2 minutes. Stir in the chicken stock, heavy cream, and squash and bring to a simmer. Slowly cook the soup, stirring occasionally, for 20 minutes. Remove the soup from the heat and, using an immersion blender, puree the soup until smooth. You can also blend the soup in batches in a blender or food processor.

To make the garnish, stir together the sour cream and honey in a small bowl. To serve, ladle the hot soup into warmed bowls and drizzle the top of each with the sour cream mixture. Garnish with freshly chopped tarragon.

Sherried Onion Soup with Gruyère Toast

This is an old-school soup that was served in "big city" restaurants when I was growing up. It was also the first soup that was taught to my class at The Culinary Institute. The key to making a good onion soup is to take your time when caramelizing the onions, cooking them until they have developed a golden brown color and a slight crust has formed on the bottom of the pan—that's where your flavor is. You must also use a high-quality beef stock if you want a flavorful soup. A good onion soup is an example of a classic dish that never goes out of style.

MAKES 6 SERVINGS

2 tablespoons olive oil

2 tablespoons unsalted butter

1½ pounds sweet onions, such as Vidalia or 1015, halved crosswise, then thinly sliced lengthwise

2 sprigs fresh thyme

2 bay leaves

1 teaspoon salt

½ teaspoon freshly ground black pepper

2 tablespoons all-purpose flour

1 cup sherry

5½ cups beef stock

6 slices baguette, each ¾ inch thick

¾ cup shredded Gruyère cheese

½ cup freshly grated Parmesan cheese

1 egg yolk

Heat a heavy soup pot over medium heat and add the olive oil and butter. When the butter is melted, add the onions to the pot and cook slowly, stirring occasionally, until they turn golden brown, about 30 minutes. If the bottom of the pot develops a crust and the onions begin to stick, add a little beef stock to release the crust and continue to cook the onions until done.

Add the thyme, bay leaves, salt, and pepper to the onions and cook for another 2 minutes. Add the flour and cook for another 1 minute, stirring continuously. With a whisk, stir ¾ cup of the sherry into the onions. As soon as the sherry comes to a simmer, whisk the beef stock into the onions and sherry. Bring the soup to a low simmer and slowly cook for 30 minutes, stirring occasionally.

As the soup is cooking, make the Gruyère toasts. Preheat your oven to 375°F. Arrange the baguette slices in a single layer on a baking sheet and bake until they just begin to turn light brown. Meanwhile, in a small bowl, stir together the Gruyère and Parmesan cheeses with the egg yolk. Top each of the partially toasted baguette slices with a mound of cheese. Return the toasts to the oven and bake until the cheese is melted, bubbly, and lightly browned.

Turn the heat off under the soup and add the remaining ¼ cup of sherry. Taste the soup for seasoning and make any adjustments, if needed. Remove the bay leaves. Ladle the soup into six heated crocks and top each with a warm Gruyère toast. Serve immediately.

Norma's Oyster Stew

Norma, my Port Arthur grandmother, was a great Cajun cook. Her cooking was rooted in her Louisiana heritage, and women of her generation would cook three meals a day for their families. On the surface their food was pretty simple fare, like gumbo, jambalaya, pork chops étouffée, roasted meats, and braised game, but it also had very complex, unique, and distinct flavors. My grandmother's oyster stew is an example of how Cajun cooks can make an unforgettable meal out of just a few ingredients. Some cooks use milk for this dish, but my grandmother would use heavy cream to make the stew a little richer.

MAKES 4 SERVINGS

1 pint small to medium oysters in their liquor

4 tablespoons unsalted butter

2 shallots, finely diced

¹/₄ cup thinly sliced green onions, white and green parts

¹/₂ cup finely diced celery

¹/₄ teaspoon kosher salt

¹/₄ teaspoon white pepper

Pinch of cayenne pepper

¹/₄ cup sherry

3 cups heavy cream

2 tablespoons chopped flat-leaf parsley, for garnish

Crackers or crusty French bread and unsalted butter, for serving

Drain the oysters, reserving both the oysters and their liquor.

Heat a soup pot over medium heat and add the butter. When the butter is melted, add the shallots, green onions, and celery and cook until soft, about 3 minutes. Season the vegetables with the salt, white pepper, and cayenne. Add the sherry and turn the heat to medium-high. Cook until the volume of the sherry reduces by half.

Add the oyster liquor and cream to the pot and bring to a simmer, reducing the heat to maintain the stew at a simmer. Stir the oysters into the stew and cook until the oysters curl and are heated through, 2 to 4 minutes.

Remove from the heat and immediately ladle the stew with some of the vegetables and oysters into warmed bowls. Garnish with a little sprinkle of chopped parsley and serve with a basket of crackers or sliced crusty French bread and sweet butter.

THE SHERRY IN THIS RECIPE adds a hint of acid and sweetness, which balance out the oysters and cream. When you are ready to serve, just reheat it and add the oysters.

Curried Chicken and Potato Stew

Every Wednesday a group of friends and I get together for a potluck dinner. Often I'll test out new dishes for the restaurant on them; all of my friends love to eat, and nobody is afraid to voice an opinion about my cooking. Otherwise, I'll throw together something easy at the last minute, like this curried chicken stew. This is one of those one-pot meals that tastes better the next day served as leftovers. You can substitute the chicken with turkey—the day after Thanksgiving, for instance—or turn it into a seafood curry by adding shrimp and fish to the curry base in the last 5 minutes of cooking.

MAKES 6 SERVINGS

1 cooked whole chicken, 3½ to 4 pounds, roasted or poached

2 tablespoons olive oil

1 small white onion, diced small

3 cloves garlic, minced

3 tablespoons minced fresh ginger

½ serrano chile, stemmed, seeded, and diced small

2 plum tomatoes, cored and diced small

3 tablespoons curry powder

1 tablespoon sugar

2 teaspoons kosher salt

1 teaspoon freshly ground black pepper

1 (13.5-ounce) can coconut milk

1 cup heavy cream

1 cup chicken stock

1 tablespoon soy sauce

1 large russet potato, peeled and diced medium

2 tablespoons coarsely chopped fresh basil

4 green onions, white and green parts, thinly sliced

¼ cup coarsely chopped cilantro, plus more for garnish

Juice of 1 lime

Cooked white rice or your favorite egg noodles, for serving

Skin and bone the cooked chicken, and cut the meat into large bite-size pieces.

Heat a large soup pot over medium-high heat and add the olive oil. Add the onion and sauté until it is soft and just begins to develop color. Add the garlic, ginger, and serrano chile and continue to cook for 1 minute more. Stir in the diced tomatoes and cook until the tomatoes soften and collapse, about 2 minutes.

Add the curry powder, sugar, salt, and black pepper to the pot and stir into the onions. Add the coconut milk, cream, stock, and soy sauce and bring to a simmer. Add the chicken meat, potato, basil, green onions, and cilantro and continue to simmer until the potatoes are tender, about 20 minutes.

Just before you serve the stew, add the juice of 1 lime to the pot. Ladle the stew over rice or noodles and garnish with a little chopped cilantro before serving.

New Mexico Pork and Green Chile Stew

New Mexico green chiles can be used in any recipe that calls for roasted chiles, such as salsas, chiles rellenos, and casseroles. My favorite—and the all-time classic—New Mexico dish is a pork and green chile stew. A big bowl full is great as a main course with some hot tortillas, or it can be used as a filling for enchiladas, burritos, and tacos. The heat of green chiles varies, depending on their variety and the season, so taste them before you add them to the stew. If you're a little shy and tender of tongue, you can pull back on how many you use. If you grew up eating these tasty peppers, you can add a few more than the recipe calls for.

MAKES 8 TO 10 SERVINGS

4 pounds pork butt, excess fat trimmed and cut into 1¹/₂-inch dice

1 tablespoon kosher salt

2 teaspoons freshly ground black pepper

3 tablespoons olive oil

2 medium yellow onions, diced small

8 cloves garlic, minced

3 plum tomatoes, cored and diced medium

2 teaspoons ground cumin

¹/₄ cup coarsely chopped cilantro

1 tablespoon coarsely chopped fresh oregano, or 1 teaspoon dried oregano

3 pounds (about 12 to 15) New Mexico green chiles, roasted, peeled, seeded, and finely diced

4 cups chicken stock

2 medium russet potatoes, peeled and cut into ¹/₂-inch dice

2 tablespoons cornmeal

Hot corn tortillas, for serving

Place the diced pork butt in a large mixing bowl and toss with the salt and pepper to season evenly. Heat a heavy saucepan over high heat and add the olive oil. Add the pork and sear to a golden brown on all sides. With a slotted spoon, transfer the pork from the pan to a platter.

Turn the heat to medium-high, add the onions, and cook until soft, about 3 minutes. Add the garlic to the pan and continue cooking for another 1 to 2 minutes, being careful not to brown the garlic. Add the tomatoes, cumin, cilantro, and oregano and stir to combine.

Add the roasted green chiles, chicken stock, and browned pork to the pan and bring to a simmer. Cover the pan and slowly simmer until the pork is tender, 2 to 2¹/₂ hours, occasionally stirring the stew and adding a little water to keep the pork covered with liquid, if needed.

When the pork reaches your desired degree of doneness (I like mine almost falling apart), add the potatoes, then sprinkle the cornmeal into the pan while stirring. The cornmeal will slightly thicken the stew and give it a sweet corn flavor. Cook until the potatoes are tender, 15 to 20 minutes.

Dish up big bowls of the stew and serve with plenty of hot tortillas.

IN FACT, NEW MEXICO LEADS THE NATION IN CHILE PRODUCTION, growing hundreds of varieties annually. The New Mexico green chile—cousin of the Anaheim—is the most iconic of all their chiles, and the Hatch green is the most sought after. The climate and terrain of the Hatch region, in the southern part of the state, give this chile its distinctive flavor.

Port Arthur Seafood Gumbo

At the heart of any good gumbo is a dark roux. Slowly cooking the flour to a nutty brown color is what gives gumbo its distinct Cajun flavor. Gumbo cooks all have their own secret seasoning mix; some are peppery hot while others are sweet and aromatic. I think my seasoning mix, like my grandmother's, strikes a good balance between the two. The stock you use in your gumbo is what will take it from good to great, as it will for any soup or stew. Gumbo filé, which is made from ground sassafras leaves, should only be added after the gumbo is finished cooking. High heat will cause the filé to become tough and stringy.

MAKES 8 TO 10 SERVINGS

2 cups medium-diced yellow onions

1½ cups medium-diced green bell peppers

1½ cups medium-diced celery

1 cup thinly sliced green onions, white and green parts

2 tablespoons Old Bay Seasoning

2 bay leaves

2 teaspoons kosher salt

1 teaspoon freshly ground black pepper

½ teaspoon white pepper

⅛ teaspoon cayenne pepper

½ teaspoon dried thyme

½ teaspoon dried oregano

Pinch of ground cloves

¾ cup vegetable oil

1 cup all-purpose flour

6 cups shrimp or chicken stock

2 cloves garlic, minced

½ cup chopped flat-leaf parsley

1½ pounds medium shrimp, peeled and deveined

1 pint medium oysters in their liquor

¾ pound crabmeat, picked over for bits of shell

4 cups cooked white rice

Crusty French bread, for serving

Hot sauce, for serving

Filé, for serving

In a large bowl, combine the yellow onions, bell peppers, celery, and ½ cup of the green onions (set aside the remaining ½ cup of green onions). In another bowl, mix together Old Bay Seasoning, bay leaves, salt, black and white pepper, cayenne, thyme, oregano, and cloves to the make the spice mix.

Heat a heavy saucepan over medium-high heat and add the vegetable oil. Stir in the flour to make a smooth roux. Turn the heat to medium and cook the roux, stirring frequently, until it slowly turns to a deep nutty-brown color, about 30 minutes. While you are cooking the roux, pour the shrimp stock into a large soup pot and begin heating it to a simmer.

Add the onion, bell pepper, and celery mixture to the roux and stir to combine, cooking for about 2 minutes. Stir in the garlic and the spice mixture—the ingredients will come together in a sticky mass—and cook for another minute while stirring.

Turn the heat up to high under the soup pot with the shrimp stock and start gradually adding the roux mixture to the stock, whisking between additions to incorporate the roux. Once all the roux has been added, bring the gumbo to a brisk simmer and cook for 15 minutes, stirring occasionally. If any foam floats to the surface of the pot, skim off with a spoon or ladle.

Add the reserved ½ cup of green onions, the parsley, and shrimp to the simmering gumbo and cook for 3 minutes. From this point on, avoid heating the mixture any higher than a simmer to keep from overcooking the seafood. Next, stir in the oysters with their liquor and continue cooking at a low simmer for another 1 minute. To finish the gumbo, gently stir in the crabmeat.

Serve immediately, mounding about $^1/_4$ cup of cooked rice in the middle of each bowl and ladling the gumbo over the top, making sure that everyone gets some shrimp and oysters. Serve with crusty French bread, passing a bottle of hot sauce and the filé at the table.

MY FATHER GREW UP IN PORT ARTHUR, TEXAS, home to the largest Cajun population outside Louisiana. As kids, my brothers and sister and I loved going to see our relatives in Port Arthur over the holidays. Visiting Port Arthur was like going to a foreign land for a boy from the ranching country of West Texas: they all spoke a broken Cajun French, drank dark chicory coffee, and spent their days fishing and crabbing. We would go to the docks and buy shrimp, oysters, and crabs from the boat, which my grandmother would make into a big pot of seafood gumbo.

There are a lot of gumbo variations. You can add andouille sausage to a seafood gumbo, make a fantastically rich wild duck gumbo, serve a light summer squash and corn gumbo, or make my favorite Sunday night dinner, a simple chicken and okra gumbo. To this day, whenever I make a pot of gumbo I think of my grandmother.

[Dark Roux]

Dark roux is used in Cajun and Creole cooking both as a thickening agent and to give sauces and soups a distinct nutty flavor. Like white and blond roux, dark roux is made by cooking flour in a fat. Usually a vegetable oil is used, because its higher smoke point stands up to the longer cooking time necessary to make a dark roux. The darker the roux, the less thickening power it has in a liquid. A dark roux has about one-fourth the thickening ability as a white one.

Over the years, I've tried many different methods for making a dark roux. The traditional way—the way my grandmother did it—is to slowly cook the flour and fat over moderate heat for about 30 minutes, constantly stirring, until the roux is a chocolate-reddish brown. Paul Prudhomme, the king of Cajun cooking, makes a quick roux by first getting the oil smoking hot and then gradually whisking in the flour before cooking it over high heat. (For years, my father tried perfecting a roux in the microwave oven; I never understood that one—sorry, Dad). I've even seen competent chefs toast the flour in the oven before adding it to the fat. When it comes down to it, the traditional way is the best (my father has even unplugged his microwave). A couple of notes: Roux is like napalm; if it gets on your skin, it will burn the dickens out of you, so be careful while stirring. If you see a couple of black specs in the roux while you are cooking it, chances are you have burned some of the flour. Even a little burn will ruin the entire roux. Throw it out and start over.

Seafood Posole Verde

Posole is the Mexican name for hominy, and also the name for this great hominy-based soup. Traditionally, posole is made with pork, hominy, and dried red chiles, but when I am using seafood in my posole, I opt for a lighter and more fragrant broth using green chiles. This recipe calls for shrimp and whitefish, but don't hesitate to add scallops and crab. Posole verde also works great as a base for chicken soup, with a little fresh baby spinach added to each bowl. If you or your guests are afraid of a little heat, you can omit the jalapeño and serve some chiles on the side.

MAKES 6 SERVINGS

2 poblano, Anaheim, or New Mexico chiles, roasted, peeled, seeded, and coarsely chopped

½ cup chopped cilantro

1 tablespoon olive oil

1 small white onion, finely chopped

1 medium Mexican squash or zucchini, diced small

1 small jalapeño, seeded and finely chopped

3 cloves garlic, minced

2 teaspoons coarsely chopped fresh oregano leaves, or 1 teaspoon dried oregano

1 teaspoon kosher salt

4 cups fish or chicken stock

1 (15-ounce) can white hominy, drained and rinsed

1 pound medium shrimp, peeled and deveined

1 pound firm whitefish fillets, such as halibut, snapper, or redfish, cut into 1-inch pieces

Juice of 1 lime

GARNISHES

2 tablespoons cilantro

2 limes, quartered

6 radishes, julienned

¼ cup finely diced white onion

1 tablespoon dried oregano

1 tablespoon red pepper flakes

Combine the roasted poblanos and ¼ cup of the cilantro in a blender and puree until smooth. Set aside.

Heat a heavy soup pot over medium-high heat and add the olive oil. Add the onion, squash, and jalapeño to the pot and cook until the onion is translucent, about 3 minutes. Add the garlic and cook for 1 minute. Add the oregano and salt, and then add the stock, pureed poblanos, and hominy. Bring to a simmer and add the remaining ¼ cup of cilantro.

With the soup at a strong simmer, stir in the shrimp and fish and allow the seafood to cook through for 5 minutes. Do not let the soup go higher than a simmer to keep the seafood from becoming overcooked and tough. Add the juice of 1 lime to the pot and taste for seasoning.

Ladle the soup into warm bowls, making sure everyone gets an equal amount of the seafood and hominy. Divide the garnishes evenly among six small plates so that each guest can season their posole to their taste.

[Hominy]

Hominy is dried corn kernels that have been hulled and stripped of their bran and germ, either by soaking in a lye solution or by mechanically cracking the corn kernels. In the South, hominy is eaten whole in the place of potatoes or rice, and it is ground into corn grits, which are eaten for breakfast, lunch, and dinner. Tom Perini, a world-renowned Texas chef and camp cook, serves hominy baked with cream and green peppers and topped with cheese and bacon—yum, yum! In Mexico and the Southwest hominy is called *posole* and used in soups and stews. Hominy is sold either canned or dried. White hominy is made from white corn kernels, and the sweeter yellow hominy is made from yellow corn kernels.

West Texas Venison Chili

When I was growing up in West Texas, after we went deer hunting we would have most of the meat ground into sausage and chili meat. Venison, which is very lean, is perfect for slowly cooking down with chili powder, cumin, and onions. It imparts a rich, mild, earthy flavor when blended with traditional chili seasonings.

MAKES 6 TO 8 SERVINGS

¼ cup vegetable oil

3 pounds coarsely ground venison or beef

2 large yellow onions, diced medium

6 cloves garlic, minced

½ cup chili powder

2 tablespoons paprika

1 tablespoon ground cumin

1 teaspoon dried oregano

2 teaspoons kosher salt

1 tablespoon freshly ground black pepper

1 teaspoon sugar

4 plum tomatoes, cored and diced medium

2 tablespoons tomato paste

1 (12-ounce) bottle of beer

1 cup water

2 tablespoons cornmeal

1 cup shredded cheddar cheese

1 cup finely diced yellow onion

Heat a large, heavy soup pot over medium heat and add the oil. Add the venison and cook until it begins to brown, about 8 minutes. Add the onion and garlic and cook until the onion becomes soft, 2 minutes.

Stir in the chili powder, paprika, cumin, oregano, salt, pepper, and sugar and cook until all of the meat is coated with the spices, about 2 minutes. Add the tomatoes, tomato paste, beer, and water and bring the chili to a simmer. Cook the chili at a low simmer for 45 minutes to 1 hour or until the flavors come together and the texture thickens. During the cooking, add water to keep the chili moist as the liquid evaporates.

At the end of the cooking time, sprinkle the cornmeal over the chili and stir in. Cook until the cornmeal is cooked through and has slightly thickened the chili, 10 to 15 minutes.

Ladle the hot chili into warm bowls and top with cheddar cheese and diced onion.

IN ITS PUREST FORM, TEXAS CHILI is made of meat, ground chiles, cumin, salt and pepper, onion, and some garlic, with a little water to wet it down. My friends from up north, check over the ingredients one more time: nowhere on the list are beans mentioned (or, for that matter, bell peppers, olives, corn, basil, or any other crazy things that some people think belong in a chili). But who am I to tell you how to make your chili? If you're happy, I'm happy.

Chili powder is the key seasoning in this dish, so if you use a quality chili powder you will end up with a quality bowl of chili. Like a lot of chili cooks, I add a little tomato to give the chili a bit more depth. Keep in mind, though, that we're making chili and not spaghetti sauce, so don't overdo the tomato. Texas chili is usually finished with a sprinkle of corn masa or cornmeal. This helps to slightly thicken the chili while giving it a hint of corn sweetness. If you must add beans to your chili, proper chili etiquette dictates that you serve them on the side, like a garnish. Let your guests decide if they want to go down that slippery slope of adding beans to their chili.

[Chili Powder]

Chili powder, or chili blend, is usually made up of ground dried red chiles, cumin, oregano, garlic, and salt. Some chili powders may also contain dried onion, black pepper, coriander, clove, or cinnamon; each manufacturer uses its own blend. There are countless different kinds of dried red chiles and combinations of seasonings that can go into chili powders. That's why it's important to buy a high-quality chili powder and not to be afraid to test different blends until you find your favorite.

Better yet, make your own chili powder blend. My favorites types of dried chiles are ancho, cascabel, guajillo, New Mexico red, and arbol. I will buy these chiles preground and mix two or three of them with a little ground cumin and oregano—and nothing else. I use my chili blend for seasoning beans and stews and for mixing with my dry rubs for seasoning meats.

A great source for ground and whole chiles and chili powders, Pendery's of Fort Worth, Texas, claims to be the originator of commercially blended chili powder. (Visit www.penderys.com.)

SAUSAGES, PÂTÉS & CURED MEATS

I FIRST LEARNED ABOUT CHARCUTERIE—the fancy French word is derived from the words *chair cuite,* which mean "cooked meats" in English—while I worked at Postrio in San Francisco. Sure, I had butchered deer and *cabrito* while growing up, and had smoked my share of beef and pork for weekend barbecues, but I had never known the reasoning behind the art of processing and cooking meats. David Gingrass, Postrio's chef (along with his wife, Annie, and Wolfgang Puck) was a fanatic when it came to making charcuterie. The restaurant made fresh and dried sausages, pâtés, galantines, ballotines, and rillettes; cured their own hams and bacon; and processed their own smoked fish. So, when I was transferred to the butcher and charcuterie shop, I looked at it as a challenge and a great opportunity to learn. Not a lot of restaurants take the time and expense to make in-house charcuterie items.

What I quickly learned was that charcuterie, like baking, is both a science and an art. The science is that each item is created by combining meat with spices and seasoning and then changing the meat's protein composition physically and/or chemically—by grinding, emulsifying, curing, cooking, or smoking. You have to follow the proper method and use the correct ratio of salt, spices, fat, and/or liquid to end up with something that is palatable. For that reason, measurements are often listed by weight instead of volume. The art of it is that you have to develop a sense of how the item you are preparing should look, feel, smell, and taste at every stage of the process. Now, not everyone can develop this sense. I know a lot of great chefs who are terrible bakers. Sure, they can follow a recipe and understand the science behind baking, but they just don't have the ability to look at or touch a dough while it is being mixed and know when it has been kneaded for the right amount of time. The same holds true for preparing charcuterie.

There is culinary magic in perfectly constructed and cooked sausages and pâtés, not the overprocessed, chemical-laden stuff you buy in the supermarket, but the handcrafted, flavorful links and loaves you can still get around the country. Hotlinks with a smoky chile punch from a hole-in-the-wall barbecue shack. Panfried fennel and red pepper-studded Italian sausage from a neighborhood deli. A chunky country pâté studded with pistachios from the little café on the corner. These uniquely American sausages and pâtés all have their roots in the region and the heritage of the people who make and serve them.

Charcuterie kitchens also prepare a wide assortment of smoked and cured meat and seafood specialties. We brine-cure legs of lamb and *cabrito* in pastrami spices and then tie and smoke them for some outrageously great sandwiches. When I want to act a little more civilized, I'll make a goose liver mousseline or some Cajun pickled shrimp. For Sunday brunch, we at Lambert's always have sides of Hot Smoked Pecan-Cured Salmon (page 67)—sweet and salty from the cure, with an earthy pecan crust. Don't let the word *charcuterie* scare you. I hope that these recipes inspire you to grind up some meat and spices and fire up the smoker.

Maple and Fennel Breakfast Sausage

Sausage patties are my meat of choice when it comes to breakfast. When they are panfried in a heavy skillet, the outside becomes nice and crisp and the inside plump with the right ratio of meat to fat. This recipe for maple and fennel sausage has a perfect balance of heat from the red pepper flakes, sweetness from the maple sugar, and depth from toasted and ground fennel seeds.

MAKES 2^1/$_2$ POUNDS

2 pounds pork butt, cut into 2-inch dice

^{1}/$_2$ pound pork fatback, cut into 1-inch dice

1 tablespoon kosher salt

1 teaspoon freshly ground black pepper

2 teaspoons fennel seeds, toasted and coarsely ground

2 tablespoons maple sugar

^{1}/$_4$ teaspoon cayenne pepper

^{1}/$_2$ teaspoon red pepper flakes

Vegetable oil, for cooking

Combine the pork butt and fatback in a metal bowl. In a small mixing bowl, combine the salt, black pepper, fennel seeds, maple sugar, cayenne, and red pepper flakes. Thoroughly stir the seasoning mixture into the diced meat and place in the freezer for 20 minutes to chill.

Set up your meat grinder with a small die. Remove the chilled meat from the freezer and grind the meat into a mixing bowl. Work the meat with your hands, kneading and squeezing it between your fingers, until it is well combined and sticky, about 2 minutes. Form the meat into 3-inch patties. The patties can be frozen for up 3 months or kept in the refrigerator for up to several days. When you're ready to serve the sausage, heat a skillet over medium heat and coat the bottom of the pan with oil. Cook the patties on both sides until crispy and golden, about 5 minutes, depending on their thickness. Serve immediately.

BREAKFAST SAUSAGE PATTIES are a great place to start learning the tricks and nuances of sausage making. All you need is a meat grinder, a hot skillet, and some hungry folks. Some eggs and buttermilk biscuits with homemade jam wouldn't hurt, either.

[Toasting Spices]

To toast spices, I spread them out on a baking sheet in a single layer and place in a 350°F oven for 5 to 8 minutes. When they just begin to develop color and release oils and aroma, I know they're ready. If I'm doing a small batch of spices, the easiest way to toast them is in a small skillet or sauté pan. Put the spices in a pan over medium-low heat and gentle shake the spices—much like popcorn—until they develop a little color, start to lightly pop, and begin to release oils and aroma, about 2 to 4 minutes. Now you're ready to grind the spices or crush them with a mortar and pestle to use in your recipe.

Chicken Sausage with Parmesan and Sun-Dried Tomatoes

We combine chicken with fennel, Parmesan, basil, and tomato, making a sausage perfect for serving alongside a big plate of pasta. When making chicken sausage we always use leg and thigh meat, because the dark meat has a little more fat than the breast and produces a better texture in the finished product. At the restaurant, we poach all our sausages right after we assemble them and then we chill them and, at serving time, finish them on the grill before presenting them. Not only does it extend the life of the sausages—cooked ones will last longer than raw ones—but it's easier to grill a cooked sausage than a raw one since the grill's high heat can break the emulsion or cause the casing to burst. Serve these sausages on a griddled hot dog bun, if you like, or slice them for nibbling with some spicy mustard and a cold beer.

MAKES 5 POUNDS

3 pounds chicken leg and thigh meat, cut into 2-inch pieces

2 pounds pork butt, cut into 2-inch pieces

1 ounce (or 2 tablespoons) kosher salt

1 tablespoon finely ground black pepper

1 tablespoon fennel seeds, toasted and ground

2 teaspoons sugar

1 teaspoon red pepper flakes

1/8 teaspoon freshly grated nutmeg

1/2 cup loosely packed fresh basil, thinly sliced

6 ounces Parmesan cheese, cut into 1/4-inch cubes

4 ounces sun-dried tomatoes, thinly sliced

1/2 cup cold chicken stock

4 ounces hog middle casings

Combine the chicken meat with the pork in a mixing bowl. In another small bowl, combine the salt, black pepper, fennel, sugar, pepper flakes, and nutmeg to make a spice blend. Sprinkle the spice blend over the meat and stir to evenly coat the meat. Place the meat in the freezer for 20 minutes to thoroughly chill.

Set up your meat grinder with a medium die and grind the chilled chicken and pork mixture into the bowl of your stand mixer. Add the basil, Parmesan, sun-dried tomatoes, and chicken stock and, using the paddle attachment, mix the sausage on medium speed for 2 minutes, until the sausage comes together into a sticky mass. If you don't have a mixer, you can work the sausage by hand in a large mixing bowl by kneading and squeezing the meat between your fingers. Keep the sausage meat refrigerated until you are ready to put it into the casings.

To prepare the casings, soak them in cold water for about 5 minutes, then flush out the inside of the casings with more cold water (like you'd fill a water balloon as a kid). Stuff the casings with the sausage meat according to your stuffer's instructions. Tie off the sausages with butcher's twine to create links 6 inches long.

To poach the sausages, bring a large pot of water to a low simmer on the stove. Attach a deep-frying thermometer to the

(continued on next page)

(Chicken Sausage with Parmesan and
Sun-Dried Tomatoes, continued)

pot. Add the sausages to the water and poach them, adjusting the heat as necessary to maintain the water temperature at 180°F to 190°F, until an instant-read thermometer inserted in the middle of the one of the sausages reaches 165°F, about 30 minutes. Carefully remove the sausages from the water and transfer to a large bowl of ice water to stop the cooking. After the sausages have cooled down in the ice bath, separate and dry the links. The sausage can now be stored in the refrigerator for up to 5 days.

To serve the sausages, grill over a medium-hot fire until the sausages are slightly charred on the outside and heated through, about 15 minutes.

Jalapeño and Cheddar Beef Hotlinks

This is the recipe for our house hotlinks at Lambert's in Austin, which we grind, stuff, and smoke, all in-house. The jalapeño gives them just the right amount of heat, and the cheddar gives them an added depth of flavor.

MAKES 5 POUNDS

2¹/₂ pounds pork butt, cut into 2-inch dice

2¹/₂ pounds beef chuck, cut into 2-inch dice

¹/₄ cup kosher salt

2 tablespoons chili powder

2 tablespoons paprika

1 tablespoon red pepper flakes

1 tablespoon freshly ground black pepper

1 tablespoon sugar

2 teaspoons onion powder

2 teaspoons garlic powder

1 teaspoon dried oregano

2 jalapeños, stemmed, seeded, and finely diced

6 ounces cheddar cheese, cut into ¹/₄-inch dice

³/₄ cup cold Lone Star beer (or your favorite brand)

4 ounces hog casings

Combine the pork and beef in a shallow container that will fit in your freezer. In a small mixing bowl, combine the salt, chili powder, paprika, red pepper flakes, black pepper, sugar, onion powder, garlic powder, and oregano. Thoroughly stir the seasoning mixture into the cubed meat and place in the freezer for 20 minutes to chill.

Bring a small pot of water to a boil. Blanch the diced jalapeños in the boiling water for about 30 seconds to set their color and lightly cook through. Drain the peppers, transfer to a small bowl, and place in the refrigerator to chill.

Set up your meat grinder with a medium die. Remove the chilled meat from the freezer and grind the meat into a large mixing bowl. Add the chilled jalapeños, diced cheddar, and beer. Work the meat with your hands by kneading and squeezing it between your fingers until the mixture comes together in a sticky mass, 2 to 3 minutes. If you have a stand mixer large enough, your can mix on medium speed for 1 minute with the paddle attachment instead. Store in the refrigerator until you are ready to stuff the casings.

To prepare the casings, soak them in cold water for 5 minutes, then flush out the inside of the casings with more cold water (like you'd fill a water balloon as a kid). Stuff the casings with the sausage meat according to your stuffer's instructions. Tie off the sausages with butcher's twine to the desired length (we produce 8-inch hotlinks).

Preheat your smoker to about 225°F. Place the sausages in the smoker in a single layer, away from the heat source, making sure that none are touching. Smoke the sausages until an instant-read thermometer inserted in one of them reaches 165°F, about 1 hour. If you are not serving the sausages immediately, transfer them to the refrigerator to stop the cooking and keep them from drying out. When you are ready to serve the sausages, heat them through on a medium-hot grill until the outsides are a little crispy and the insides are hot.

NOT THAT LONG AGO it was customary for every self-respecting barbecue joint, shack, or restaurant to make its own hotlinks. Some were spicy hot with cayenne pepper, some were sweet with a hint of cumin and fennel, and some had an artificial red glow reminiscent of a famous reindeer's nose. All, though, were a fatty, flavorful calling card of the pit boss, as individual as his rubs, barbecue sauce, and the degree of smoke on his brisket and ribs. Nowadays, however, washed-out country singers and over-the-hill football players are lending their names to mass-produced sausages that are being passed off as Texas hotlinks. Take it from me, you want to find the real deal: sausages that are fresh and made from scratch.

[Sausage Casings]

Sausages come in a variety of shapes, sizes, and flavors. Common to all of them is that spiced and seasoned sausage meat has been stuffed into a casing. Casings can either be natural or manufactured, edible or not, and ranging in sizes from small to large.

Natural casings come from the intestines of sheep, hogs, or beef, and are the preferred casings of most sausage makers because of the strength and elasticity, superiority in smoking, and flavor and mouth feel. For the sausages that we make at Lambert's—grilled, smoked, and poached—natural hog casings work best.

Hog casings are made from the small intestine of the animal. When hogs are processed, the casing are flushed out, sanitized and packed in a salt solution to preserve them. We purchase commercial hog casings in a hank (that's 300 feet of casings). Hog casings are readily available in specialty markets and by mail order (see Sources, page 252). You will need about 2 feet of casings per 1 pound of sausage you're making.

Spicy Oak-Smoked Chorizo

Spanish chorizo is a traditional smoked and cured pork sausage, seasoned with dried red peppers, whereas Mexican chorizo, made with pork, chiles, and garlic, is as a raw sausage. This recipe works great for both: it can be used like a Mexican chorizo, cooked from its raw state, or you can stuff the sausage into casings and smoke it, like a Spanish chorizo. Use the chorizo to punch up flavors in soups, pastas, stuffing, or even your morning scrambled eggs. You can control the amount of heat in this recipe by pulling back on the amount of chili powder and red pepper flakes in the sausage.

MAKES 5 POUNDS

5 pounds pork butt, cut into 2-inch cubes

1 ounce (2 tablespoons) kosher salt

1 tablespoon finely ground black pepper

1 tablespoon sugar

2 tablespoons chili powder

2 tablespoons paprika

2 teaspoons red pepper flakes

1 teaspoon dried oregano

1/2 teaspoon ground allspice

8 cloves garlic, minced

1/4 cup cider vinegar

1/2 cup cold water

4 ounces hog casings

Place the pork butt in a large mixing bowl. In a small mixing bowl, combine the salt, black pepper, sugar, chili powder, paprika, red pepper flakes, oregano, and allspice. Stir the spice mixture into the pork, evenly coating the meat, and place in the freezer for 20 minutes to chill.

Set up your meat grinder with a medium die. Grind the cold pork into the bowl of your stand mixer. Add the vinegar and water and, using the paddle attachment, mix the ground pork on medium speed for 3 minutes until the sausage comes together in a uniform sticky mass. If you don't have a mixer, you can mix the sausage by hand in a large mixing bowl by kneading and squeezing the meat through your fingers. Refrigerate the sausage while you prepare the sausage casings for stuffing.

To prepare the casings, first soak them in cold water for about 5 minutes, then flush out the inside of the casings with more cold water. Stuff the casings with sausage meat according to your stuffer's directions and tie off the sausages with butcher's twine (we produce 6-inch chorizos).

Preheat your smoker to about 225°F. Place the sausages in the smoker in a single layer, away from the heat source, making sure that none are touching. Smoke until an instant-read thermometer inserted in one of the sausages reaches 170°F, 45 minutes to 1 hour. If you are not serving the sausages immediately, transfer them to the refrigerator to stop the cooking and keep them from drying out. When you are ready to serve the sausages, heat them through on a medium grill until the outsides are a little crispy and the insides are hot.

Brandied Chicken Liver Terrine with Caramelized Onions

Chicken livers: you either love them or hate them. I've always loved them, finding the creamy and earthy flavor both comforting and a little exotic at the same time. As kids, my brother and I would order them at Leslie's Fried Chicken, a place next to my dad's office on Dixie Boulevard in Odessa. I was first turned on to chopped chicken livers in San Francisco by a Jewish coworker from New Jersey. He would have his mother send him chopped chicken livers and pastrami from his neighborhood delicatessen when he got homesick. Here's my version, great for an afternoon snack or a little nosh when entertaining.

MAKES 10 TO 12 SERVINGS

1 pound chicken livers

6 tablespoons unsalted butter, at room temperature

1 cup small-diced yellow onions

Kosher salt and finely ground black pepper

2 tablespoons brandy

1 hard-boiled egg, finely diced

1 tablespoon thinly sliced chives

Toast points or crusty bread, for serving

Rinse the chicken livers under running water and pat dry. Trim any excess fat or membranes from the livers and set them aside.

In a large skillet over medium-high heat, add 2 tablespoons of the butter to the pan. Add the onions and lightly season with salt and pepper. Sauté until the onions are soft and nicely browned, about 5 minutes. Transfer to a plate to cool. Wipe out the sauté pan and add another 2 tablespoons of the butter. Season the chicken livers with salt and pepper and add them to the pan in a single layer (you may have to cook them in two batches). After the livers are lightly browned, 2 to 3 minutes, turn them over and cook the second side. When the second side is browned, add the brandy to the pan and let it reduce by half. Transfer the livers and the juices from the pan to a bowl to cool, uncovered, in the refrigerator for 15 minutes.

Combine the onions, livers, and the remaining 2 tablespoons of butter in your food processor. Pulse the machine a few times until the livers and onions are coarsely chopped. Add the chopped livers and onions to a mixing bowl, add the chopped egg, and stir to combine. Stir in the chives and taste, adjusting the seasoning, if needed. Transfer the chopped livers to a lightly oiled terrine. Allow the terrine to cool in the refrigerator for at least an hour. Serve in the terrine with toast points as a snack or spread on crusty bread for a great sandwich.

Hunters' Country Venison Pâté

This is a classic country pâté made with venison and pork. Venison is a very lean meat, so pork butt is added to give the pâté enough fat to make it tasty and moist. If you can't get venison, this recipe also works great with a leg of lamb. Serve with crusty bread, sliced onions, a good mustard, and cold beer.

MAKES 16 TO 18 SERVINGS

3 pounds venison, cut into 2-inch dice

2 pounds pork butt, cut into 2-inch dice

¹/₄ cup kosher salt

1 tablespoon freshly ground black pepper

2 teaspoons coriander seeds, toasted and ground

2 teaspoons fennel seeds, toasted and ground

1 tablespoon paprika

1 teaspoon red pepper flakes

1 tablespoon olive oil, plus more for the baking dish

2 shallots, coarsely chopped

3 cloves garlic, coarsely chopped

3 fresh sage leaves, coarsely chopped

¹/₂ cup dry red wine

4 slices bacon

Place the venison and pork butt in a large mixing bowl or pan that will fit in your freezer. In a smaller bowl, mix the salt, black pepper, coriander, fennel, paprika, and red pepper flakes to make a spice mix. Add the spice mix to the meat, tossing to coat all of the pieces. Place the seasoned meat in the freezer until thoroughly chilled, about 20 minutes.

Heat a small sauté pan over medium-high heat and add the olive oil. Cook the shallot, garlic, and sage until the shallot is cooked through and garlic just begins to develop color. Add the red wine to the pan and cook until the wine is reduced by about half. Transfer the wine mixture to a bowl and place in the refrigerator to cool.

Preheat your oven to 325°F.

Set up your meat grinder with a medium die. Remove the chilled meat from the freezer and stir in the chilled wine mixture. Grind the meat into the bowl of your stand mixer. Using the paddle attachment, mix on medium speed for 3 minutes until the mixture comes together in a sticky mass. If you don't have a mixer, you can work the meat with your hands in a large mixing bowl by kneading and squeezing the meat between your fingers for about 4 minutes.

Lightly brush the inside of a 9 by 5-inch loaf pan with oil. Tightly pack the meat in the pan, banging the pan on the counter to release any air pockets. Top the pâté with the bacon slices and then wrap the top of the pan with aluminum foil.

Place the loaf pan in the middle of a roasting pan and pour hot water into the roasting pan until it comes about halfway up the side of the loaf pan. Bake the pâté until an instant-read thermometer inserted in the middle reaches 165°F, about 1 hour. Place the cooked pâté in the refrigerator and let cool for at least 4 hours. Remove the pâté from the pan and wipe any away excess fat. Wrap in plastic wrap and store in the refrigerator until ready to serve. The pâté holds great for about a week. To serve, cut into ¹/₂-inch slices.

I'VE BEEN HUNTING BIG MULE DEER in the Davis Mountains of West Texas and skittish whitetail deer in south Texas around Carrizo Springs throughout my life. Over the years, it has become less important to me if I actually take a deer; it's more about the fall ritual of loading up the truck with all my gear and getting out of the city with my buddies that's important to me now. I am always tapped to be the camp cook, even though, year after year, I swear that the next year someone else has to take on the cooking duties. I always bring a country venison pâté along in the cooler with some crusty bread and good mustard. A slice of pâté with a cold beer is the best way I have found to keep the boys at bay while I'm cooking dinner. Truth is, I think I would be a little hurt if they found a new cook for next year.

[Sausages and Pâtés]

The first thing to understand when making sausages and pâtés is that they are an emulsion of fat, meat, spices, and liquid. An emulsion is created when two usually unblendable ingredients are forced together with some type of physical energy. The energy used to force the fat and meat together in a forcemeat emulsion is usually a stand mixer with a paddle attachment. When I am making a small batch of forcemeat, sometimes I will just mix the meat together by hand, squeezing the mixture between my fingers (like you did with mud as a kid) until it is sticky and emulsified. All emulsions are unstable, and the wrong temperature is one of the main reasons they separate, so you should always keep your ingredients as cold as possible when making a forcemeat. I always put the meat in the freezer for about 20 minutes before I grind it to make sure it is as cold as possible. Raw sausages are usually cooked either by poaching them in water or by smoking them. Either way, make sure the water and the smoker is never hotter than 190°F or you run the risk of the meat emulsion breaking. This is why we usually don't cook raw sausage directly on a hot grill. The high heat from the grill will cause the casings to break and the meat to separate and look like hamburger. Pâtés should be cooked in a moderate (300°F to 325°F) oven in a water bath. Sausages and pâtés are both cooked to an internal temperature of at least 225°F to ensure that they are safe to eat.

You might have noticed that the first ingredient I mentioned when describing making forcemeat is fat. That's because you can't make a decent sausage or pâté without enough fat. It's what binds the meat together and gives you that great velvety mouthfeel and rich fatty flavor. That is why pork butt makes great sausage: it has the perfect balance of meat and fat.

You don't have to run to the restaurant supply store and invest a chunk of money on equipment to start making your own sausages and pâtés. When I'm making them at home I still use a hand-cranked grinder I bought over twenty years ago. There is something therapeutic about clamping the grinder on the kitchen counter and grinding meat and mixing in the spices by hand to make breakfast sausage on a Saturday morning. If you don't want to use this old-school method, you can buy a grinder and sausage-stuffer combo for your stand mixer for not a lot of money. If you really want to simplify the process, you can have your butcher grind your meat for you.

Foie Gras Mousseline

Don't let the French name intimidate you, even if this is the type of dish you usually find in white-tablecloth restaurants. Foie gras, or fattened goose liver to you and me, may be expensive, but it's still just liver. We serve this mousseline in little ramekins alongside grilled sausages and local cheeses on our charcuterie board at Lambert's. It's great spread on buttery toast with some shaved onion and a cold beer or some good wine.

MAKES A 1-POUND TERRINE

1 pound grade C foie gras, cleaned and cut into 1-inch dice

4 tablespoons unsalted butter

1 tablespoon finely minced shallot

1 teaspoon finely chopped fresh thyme

Kosher salt and white pepper

¼ cup port wine

2 tablespoons heavy cream

Pinch of cayenne pepper

Clean the foie gras by pulling apart the lobe at the natural seams and removing any visible veins or membranes.

Heat a large sauté pan over medium heat and add the butter. When the butter has melted, add the shallot and thyme and cook until the shallot begins to soften, about 1 minute. Add the foie gras to the pan in a single layer, lightly season with salt and pepper, and cook about 1 minute per side, until medium-rare. Add the port and cook for another minute.

With a slotted spoon, transfer the foie gras to a metal bowl and place in the refrigerator to cool for about 5 minutes. Pour the fat from the pan through a strainer into another bowl; place in the refrigerator to cool along with the foie gras for 5 minutes.

Place the slightly cooled foie gras and half of the fat from the pan in a food processor. Add the cream and process for 1 minute, until smooth. Work the foie gras mixture through a fine-mesh strainer with a rubber spatula into a mixing bowl. Whisk in the cayenne, taste, and adjust the seasoning. Transfer the foie gras mousse to a lightly oiled terrine or ramekins and spoon remaining reserved fat over the mousse. Cover and let the mousseline chill in the refrigerator for at least 4 hours before serving.

Pecos Wild Duck Rillettes

Wild duck is perfect for rillettes, which are made by cooking and preserving meat in fat. I add a little pork to the recipe for additional fat and moisture. The duck meat is slowly cooked down in fat and spices to make the meat tender and full of flavor. I've used the same recipe and technique for making rillettes from goose, lamb, venison, rabbit, and *cabrito*. If you are buying the duck meat from the grocer, duck legs and thighs will yield more meat per pound than a whole duck.

MAKES 10 TO 12 SERVINGS

1/2 pound pork fatback or pork belly, ground or finely diced

1 cup olive oil

2 pounds duck meat, cut into 2-inch pieces

1 cup water

2 shallots, finely diced

2 cloves garlic, coarsely chopped

2 teaspoons fresh thyme

1 bay leaf

1 teaspoon kosher salt

1 teaspoon freshly ground black pepper

2 tablespoons sherry vinegar

1 tablespoon finely chopped flat-leaf parsley

Crusty bread, cornichons, and whole grain mustard, for serving

Add the pork and olive oil to a large ovenproof pot and place over medium-low heat. Cook, slowly rendering some of the pork fat into the olive oil, for 15 minutes. Add the duck meat, water, shallots, garlic, thyme, bay leaf, salt, and pepper to the pan and bring just about to a simmer (190°F), about 15 minutes. You want to slowly poach the duck, not fry it.

Preheat your oven to 275°F. Cover the pan and place in the oven. Cook, stirring about every 45 minutes, until the duck begins to flake and fall apart, 2 to 2 1/2 hours. Remove the pan from the oven and allow the duck to cool for about 15 minutes. With a slotted spoon, transfer the duck and pork to the bowl of your stand mixer. Add about half of the fat from the pan, the sherry vinegar, and parsley. With the paddle attachment, mix the duck and fat until the duck is shredded and the fat is incorporated into the meat. If you don't have a mixer, you can do the same thing by working the duck meat and fat in a mixing bowl with a wire whisk. Taste the rillettes and adjust the seasoning, if needed.

Pack the rillettes into a crock or bowl and pour a thin layer of the remaining fat over the top. Allow the rillettes to cool in the refrigerator for a couple of hours or, better yet, overnight. Serve with plenty of crusty bread, cornichons, and whole grain mustard. The rillettes will keep in the refrigerator for up to a week.

Hot Smoked Pecan-Cured Salmon

The cure for this salmon is really more like a seasoning because it's applied to the fish for only a short time. The addition of pecans adds an unexpected dimension to the sweet, smoky flavor of the fish. We serve whole fillets of this hot smoked salmon for brunch with a lemon and dill sour cream and toasted bagel chips. Any leftovers are great scrambled with eggs or panfried with potatoes and peppers for a smoked salmon hash.

MAKES 15 TO 20 SERVINGS

1 salmon fillet, 2 to 3 pounds, skin removed

¹/₄ cup kosher salt

¹/₄ cup firmly packed brown sugar

¹/₄ cup finely chopped pecans, toasted

¹/₄ cup finely chopped dill

2 teaspoons cracked black pepper

¹/₂ teaspoon red pepper flakes

Juice of 1 lemon

Pecan Salmon Glaze

Line a baking sheet with plastic wrap and place the salmon on top. Combine the salt, brown sugar, pecans, dill, black pepper, red pepper flakes, and lemon juice in a small bowl. Spread the mixture onto the salmon, smoothing it evenly over the entire surface. Cover the salmon with plastic wrap and refrigerate for 2 hours.

Remove the salmon from the refrigerator and scrape off the cure mixture, reserving the cure mix and all of the liquid on the baking sheet to use for the glaze. Cut a piece of parchment paper just slightly larger than the salmon fillet, lightly oil it, and place on a clean baking sheet. Transfer the fillet to the parchment.

Preheat your smoker to between 180°F and 200°F. Place the salmon on the baking sheet in the smoker and cook until an instant-read thermometer inserted into the middle of the salmon reaches 110°F, about 45 minutes.

Preheat your oven to 350°F. Remove the salmon from the smoker and evenly brush the pecan glaze over the top. Place the salmon in the oven and continue cooking until the salmon reaches an internal temperature of 121°F at its thickest part. Let the salmon rest for 15 minutes before removing it from the parchment paper and carefully transferring it to a platter.

PECAN SALMON GLAZE

Cure and liquid reserved from curing salmon

¹/₄ cup firmly packed brown sugar

¹/₄ cup finely chopped pecans, toasted

Put the reserved salmon cure and liquid in a small saucepan and add the brown sugar. Bring to a simmer over medium heat and cook until the sugar has melted, about 2 minutes. Strain the liquid through a fine-mesh sieve into a clean saucepan,

(continued on next page)

(Hot Smoked Pecan-Cured Salmon, continued)

discarding any solids. Return to a simmer and cook until the liquid is the consistency of heavy cream, 3 to 5 minutes more. Remove from the heat and stir in the pecans. While the glaze is still warm, brush it on top of the smoked salmon.

MY EXPOSURE TO SMOKED FISH was fairly nonexistent when I was a kid growing up in West Texas, but in my teenage years I spent most of my summers on a ranch in Colorado, outside Gunnison. There I spent all of my free time fishing for trout, with the day's catch usually ending up in a frying pan beside the creek or stream I was fishing. I would take leftovers to an old-timer who had worked as a cowboy on the ranch and who rarely went to town. He would put the fish in a salt cure for a day and then smoke the whole fish in a smoker he had rigged from an old metal refrigerator behind his shack of a house. I know this old cowboy hadn't learned this trick from going to culinary school or dining at Le Cirque in New York. He had learned, when growing up, that salting and smoking meats was an efficient and tasty way to preserve meat, and he taught me as well.

[Cured Meats]

Cooks have been curing meats since cavemen dragged pieces of meat next to the fire and let them dry out into hunks of jerky. Curing, like most of the food preparation methods we take for granted today, was an accidental discovery that has been refined over thousands of years by trial and error.

In **curing**, salt draws out moisture from the meat's cells by osmosis, which kills harmful microorganisms and inhibits spoilage. When salt curing, always use kosher salt because of its cleaner flavor. The large, irregular size of its crystals also makes it easier to mix and spread the salt on the product you're curing. When you add spices and herbs to the salt for a cure (sugar and dill for gravlax), always taste the mixture to make sure it's balanced.

Unlike a traditional salt cure, where most of the moisture is removed from the meat, **brining** makes the meat moister by hydrating the cells through the process of denaturation. Denaturation simply means that a meat's natural moisture is replaced with the salt solution in the brine. I add a little honey or brown sugar to my pork brine, pickling spices to corned beef, and black pepper and coriander to pastrami. Brining, with the addition of smoke, is what makes hams so moist, gives them their unique flavor, and makes them resist spoilage. Over time we've learned that smoked foods are just plain tasty.

Cold smoking is used to give foods a smoky flavor without actually cooking them. Because of the low temperature (below 100°F) used, foods must either be cured before smoking or cooked after smoking.

Hot smoking is exactly what it sounds like. By smoking foods at a higher temperature (185°F to 275°F), we can smoke and cook the meat at the same time.

Barbecuing or **pit roasting** is the type of smoking that most of us do on the weekend when the gang comes over for a beer and 'cue. Ribs, brisket, and pork butt are some of the hunks of meat that we love to barbecue for long periods of time, "slow and low." Even though we cook these meats "low," the temperature needs to be hotter (275°F to 350°F) than it does when hot smoking.

Pickled Cajun Shrimp

All along the Gulf Coast pickled shrimp are a summer treat, served as a snack with a little rémoulade, tossed with greens for a salad, or piled high on a French loaf as a sandwich. Around Port Arthur, Texas, a Cajun version of pickled shrimp, revved up with a touch more pepper and Old Bay Seasoning, is popular. The trick to tender shrimp is not to cook them at too high a heat or for too long; you want to poach the shrimp, not boil them.

MAKES 2 POUNDS

2 pounds large shrimp
(26 to 30 per pound),
unpeeled

COURT BOUILLON

8 cups water

¹/₄ cup white wine
vinegar

Juice of 2 lemons

¹/₂ small white onion,
thinly sliced

2 tablespoons Old Bay
Seasoning

1 bay leaf

¹/₂ teaspoon fresh
thyme

1 tablespoon kosher salt

1 teaspoon red pepper
flakes

PICKLING MARINADE

1 cup court bouillon,
from cooking shrimp

Juice of 2 lemons

1 lemon, thinly sliced
into rounds

¹/₄ cup white wine
vinegar

¹/₄ cup olive oil

1 teaspoon kosher salt

1 teaspoon sugar

3 green onions, white
and green parts, finely
chopped

2 tablespoons finely
chopped flat-leaf
parsley

Peel the shrimp, remove the tails, and devein. (Shrimp shells are great for making shrimp stock for other recipes, so store them in the freezer to use later.)

To make the court bouillon, combine all the ingredients in a large pot and bring to a simmer. Cook for 5 minutes to allow the flavors to come together.

Bring the court bouillon to a boil and add the shrimp. Once the shrimp are added to the pot, the liquid should drop to a simmer. Reduce the heat and cook the shrimp at a simmer until they are just cooked through, 3 to 5 minutes. Ladle out 1 cup of the court bouillon to use in the pickling marinade and set it aside to cool. Using a colander, drain the shrimp, then plunge the shrimp and onions into an ice bath for 1 to 2 minutes to stop the cooking. Remove the shrimp from the ice and store, covered, in the refrigerator until you are ready to pickle them.

To make the pickling marinade, stir all the ingredients together in a large bowl. Add the cooked shrimp and sliced onions to the marinade and stir to coat. Transfer the shrimp and marinade to a glass jar, cover, and refrigerate for at least 6 hours before serving. The pickled shrimp will keep in the refrigerator for up to a week.

Peppered Lamb Pastrami

I first learned to make lamb pastrami when I was working in California. As when you make beef pastrami, you start out by putting the lamb in a pickling brine for several days. A brine not only helps add moisture to the meat, but it also gives you the chance to add flavor. Once the pastrami has brined, you add more flavor to the meat with a spicy black pepper, cumin, and coriander rub and a trip through the smoker. Thinly slice pastrami for a great lamb sandwich, or serve it with some fruited mustard, grilled potatoes, and tomato wedges for a light lunch.

MAKES 8 SERVINGS

BRINE

8 cups water

1/2 cup kosher salt

1 tablespoon honey

6 cloves garlic, coarsely chopped

2 bay leaves

1 tablespoon cumin seeds, toasted

1 tablespoon coriander seeds, toasted

1 tablespoon black peppercorns, toasted

1 boneless leg of lamb, 3 to 4 pounds

DRY RUB

2 tablespoons black peppercorns, toasted

2 tablespoons coriander seeds, toasted

2 tablespoons cumin seeds, toasted

To make the brine, bring 4 cups of the water to a boil and add the salt and honey, stirring until the salt is dissolved. Add the remaining 4 cups of cold water and all the remaining brine ingredients. Transfer to a covered container and place in the refrigerator to cool completely.

Add the leg of lamb to the cold brine and place a small plate on top of the lamb to keep it submerged in the brine. Cover the container and refrigerate for 3 days.

After 3 days, remove the lamb from the brine, brush off any of the seasonings, and pat the meat dry.

Combine all of dry rub ingredients in a blender or spice grinder and coarsely grind. Dust both sides of the lamb with half of the dry rub, rubbing it into the meat with your hands. Form the leg of lamb back into its original shape (before it was boned) by pulling the two flat sides of butterflied lamb back together and tying it with 5 or 6 pieces of butcher's twine to secure it tightly. Dust the lamb with a little more of the dry rub.

Preheat your smoker to 275°F to 300°F. Hot smoke the lamb in the middle of the smoker until an instant-read thermometer inserted in the lamb reaches 140°F, about 2 hours. Allow to cool completely before thinly slicing.

BEEF, LAMB, PORK & GAME

AM A "MIDDLE OF THE PLATE" KIND OF MEAT GUY. A big pepper-crusted rib eye from the grill; roasted leg of lamb slathered with mustard and garlic; slow-smoked pork butt rubbed with chiles, salt, and coriander; braised hunter-style venison with mushrooms and caramelized onions—just give me a hunk of meat on a plate. I have to confess, though, that I'm a little biased when it comes to my meat preference. My family has been ranching beef cattle in Texas for seven generations, so it's only natural that my cooking features a lot of beef.

Beef cattle first came to North America in 1519 with Hernán Cortés, who established ranches in Mexico. These cattle often ran wild and ended up in Texas and California. Cattle from England and northern Europe began arriving in New York around 1625. As settlers began to move to the West, it was always the ranchers and cattlemen who pioneered the new country and settled the towns. By 1865, Chicago's Union Stock Yards had become the hub of the livestock industry. Two years later the railroad reached Abilene, Kansas, thus opening up the eastern markets for Texas trail herds, which started the legendary cattle drives.

Today there are 800,000 cattle operations in the United States, most of them family farms and ranches. Cattle and beef production represent the largest single segment of American agriculture. Americans, who have always romanticized the cowboy and rancher, often think of them as a thing of the past, but these hardworking men and women still saddle up their horses before daybreak, build miles of fences by hand, and worry about rain and the price of feed, just like their fathers and grandfathers before them. The reality, though, is that these folks have modernized their industry. Cattlemen are always having to react to the economic and consumer demands of the market, responding to increased fuel and feed costs, labor shortages, fluctuating beef prices, changes in the international market, and new consumer nutritional demands. Ranchers today have to be both savvy businesspeople and scientists. They have to understand the financial aspects of running a large business and how, through breeding and genetics, to control the size and quality of the cattle they take to market.

Today, when you visit your local grocer's meat counter or your favorite steak house, you almost need a degree from Texas A&M to understand what to buy. There are more cuts with different names than ever before. Not only do you have to choose the cut of meat you want, such as rib eye, tenderloin, or strip steak, but you also have to decide on natural, organic, wet aged, dry aged, Certified Angus, USDA Choice, or Bob's Best Beef. It goes on and on.

In addition to recipes for gratifying meat dishes, in this chapter you'll find a road map of sorts to take you on a guided tour of the meat world.

[Techniques]

Braising uses both moist and dry heat. I'm sure your mother cooked a killer pot roast or beef stew. **Stewing**, by the way, is a form of braising that just uses more liquid. Both start out with tough pieces of meat that are seared at a high temperature and then slowly cooked in liquid. Braising uses slow, moist heat over a long period of time to break down tough connective tissue and collagens in the meat. Meats that are braised can have a lot of external fat, like brisket and short ribs, but usually lack the internal flecks of fat that make them a good candidate for grilling and pan searing. That's okay, because braising transforms the meat from tough to tender, with the bonus of creating a rich and flavorful sauce at the same time.

We use a technique we call **smoke braising** at the restaurant. We use a technique that's similar to regular braising, but instead of pan-searing the meat, we sear it on a hot grill before slowly braising it uncovered in a hot smoker. I love to smoke braise fatty beef short ribs or a big bone-in pork butt on my backyard grill in the summertime. It takes the heat out of the kitchen and makes cleanup a lot easier when I'm having a group of friends over for an informal get-together.

Brining, or soaking meat in a salt solution, is another form of curing and flavoring using salt and osmosis. Unlike a traditional salt cure, where most of the moisture is removed from the meat, brining makes the meat moister by hydrating the cells through the process of denaturaton, which simply means that a meat's natural moisture is replaced with the salt solution in the brine. That's important to us as cooks because it gives us the opportunity to add flavor to the meat through the brine. I add a little honey or brown sugar to my pork and poultry brine, pickling spices to corned beef, and black pepper and coriander to pastrami. Brining, with the addition of smoke, is what makes meats so moist, gives them their unique flavor, and helps them resist spoilage.

Over time, we've learned that smoked foods are just plain tasty. Regardless of the fact that they won't spoil as quickly, we enjoy eating them. Who wouldn't prefer a piece of salty smoked bacon over an uncured slice of pork? Smoking produces heat, which not only decreases the internal moisture content in foods but also dries out the food's surface, which controls oxidation and spoilage. The smoke also creates a layer of hydrocarbons on the surface of the food that inhibits bacterial growth as well. So, smoking imparts flavor, helps preserve the food, and can be used to cook food.

Roasting is a pretty straightforward cooking method. You just put a big piece of meat in the oven and cook it until it is done. That's the general idea, but here are a few things to consider the next time you roast a plump chicken or beautiful beef rib roast for dinner or barbecue a brisket for the gang this weekend. Roasting is a dry heat cooking method that does a couple of things to the meat. As the meat heats, starting at the surface of the meat and working its way to the core, the proteins in the meat coagulate, or cook. The surface of the meat, which is in direct contact with the heat, browns and develops a crust through the caramelization of the natural sugars in the meat. So, as a rule, the larger the piece of meat you are roasting, the lower temperature and the longer the roasting time should be used. If you cook a 5-pound rib roast at 375°F, you will lose a lot of the weight (in fat and juices) and end up with the outside of the roast being well done by the time the inside of the roast reaches medium-rare. Tougher cuts of meat, like pork butt and beef brisket, need low and slow cooking to keep all of the juices and fat from ending up in the bottom of the roasting pan or barbecue pit. The opposite is true for small cuts of meat. It is best to roast cuts like a rack of lamb, fish, or a chicken breast at high temperature, 400°F or higher. This will ensure that you develop a good crust on the meat by the time the internal temperature is where you want it.

Barbecuing or **pit-roasting** is what most of us do on the weekend when the gang comes over for a beer and 'cue. Ribs, brisket, and pork butt are some of the chunks of meat that we love to barbecue for long periods of time, "low and slow." Even though we cook these meats "low," the temperature needs to be hotter (275°F to 350°F) than is used for hot smoking.

Adobo-Grilled T-Bone with Red Chile and Cheese Enchiladas

I came up with this combination of a T-bone with mole served with enchiladas for a party I hosted while I was in school in New York. I was homesick for West Texas and needed some food that reminded me of home. For me, this is pure big ranch cooking at its best.

MAKES 6 SERVINGS

6 (16-ounce, 1-inch-thick)
T-bone steaks

2 cups Ancho Mole Sauce
(page 246)

Kosher salt and freshly
ground black pepper

2 tablespoons unsalted
butter

Brush both sides of the steaks with some of the mole sauce and let marinate, covered, in the refrigerator for 1 to 2 hours. About 20 minutes before grilling, remove the steaks from the refrigerator to let them come to room temperature.

Start a medium-hot fire in your grill and season the grill grates with a little oil. Lightly season each side of the steaks with salt and pepper. Grill each side for 3 to 4 minutes for medium-rare. Let the steaks rest on a warm platter for about 5 minutes before serving.

While the steaks are resting, put the remaining mole in a small saucepan and bring to a simmer over medium heat. Remove the sauce from the heat and whisk in the butter 1 tablespoon at a time. Serve the steaks with the mole sauce on the side.

RED CHILE AND CHEESE ENCHILADAS   MAKES 6 SERVINGS

This type of enchilada, common at restaurants in the Austin area, is known for being served with *salsa roja,* which is made by pureeing rehydrated dried chiles with onions, garlic, tomatoes, and spices. (The more traditional Tex-Mex enchilada sauce, usually called "enchilada gravy" by cooks, is made with chili powder, spices, stock, and a roux.) I love the pungent red chile flavor of the Austin-style enchiladas balanced with the fat and creaminess of the cheese. Serve these enchiladas with some refried beans and Spanish rice, or, do like we do in our restaurant and dish them up alongside a grilled T-bone steak.

1/2 cup vegetable oil

3 1/2 cups Salsa Roja
(page 249)

12 (6-inch) corn tortillas

2 cups shredded queso
blanco

2 cups shredded
Monterey Jack cheese

3/4 cup minced yellow
onion

2 cups finely shredded
green cabbage

2 plum tomatoes, cored
and finely chopped

Preheat your oven to 350°F. Lightly oil a 9 by 13-inch glass or ceramic baking dish.

In a skillet, warm the vegetable oil over medium heat. In another skillet, warm 1/2 cup of the salsa over medium heat. Using tongs, dip each tortilla in the oil, coating both sides,

(continued on next page)

until softened, about 5 seconds. Then coat each tortilla with the salsa and transfer to a plate, stacking the tortillas on top of each other.

In a bowl, mix the queso blanco with the Monterey Jack. Set a tortilla on a work surface and spoon $1/4$ cup of the cheese mixture and about 1 tablespoon of the minced onion in the center. Loosely roll up the tortilla like a cigar and set it in the prepared baking dish, seam side down. Repeat with the remaining tortillas, cheese, and onion. Pour the remaining 3 cups salsa over the rolled enchiladas and sprinkle the remaining 1 cup of cheese on top.

Bake the enchiladas for 25 minutes, or until heated through and the sauce is bubbling. Scatter the cabbage and tomatoes over the enchiladas and serve hot.

[A Guide to Beef]

Most beef is marketed using a quality grade set by either the United States Department of Agriculture (USDA) or independent packers who establish their own quality and grading standards for the product known as Branded Beef. USDA-graded beef makes up the majority of beef we purchase in the grocery store and that is served in restaurants. USDA inspectors oversee the slaughter practices and carcass grading that take place at packing plants. The inspectors grade the carcasses and evaluate the meat's quality based on marbling (the distribution of internal flecks of fat) and the age of the animal, giving a grade of Select, Choice, or Prime. Flavor and tenderness are determined by the amount of marbling in a cut of beef and the age of the beef. Select is the leanest grade; Prime, considered the highest quality, has the highest concentration of marbling and is the most expensive. We are all trying to eat healthier and limit saturated animal fats in our diets, but the bottom line is that the fat is what gives meat its flavor and makes it tender.

Branded Beef is also processed at packing plants overseen by USDA inspectors, but it is marketed under a brand name with specific attributes for each brand, such as tenderness, health benefits, taste, and juiciness. Every Branded Beef program is unique. Most have specifications around grade, aging, and size. In general, there are three categories of Branded Beef. Breed Specific indicates cattle from a specific breed. For example, Certified Angus Beef (CAB) uses only Angus cattle for their program. Company Specific includes beef from all types of breeds but indicates other criteria such as marbling, size, types of feed used, and restrictions on the use of pesticides, antibiotics, and growth hormones. Store-Branded is the name given to the products found in some grocery store chains that now offer their own beef, in packaging produced exclusively for those stores.

Beef is also marketed according to how they were raised and what they were fed. **Grain-fed beef** is the type most widely produced in the United States today. Grain-fed cattle spend most of their lives eating grass in pastures before they move on to feedlots where they eat a high-energy grain diet for three to six months. Remember the USDA grading system: producers are trying to increase the fat and marbling in the beef to increase the yield, which increases the price they can get per pound.

Grass-finished beef comes from cattle that have been raised solely on pasture their entire lives. Grass-finished beef tends to have less marbling than grain-fed beef, and thus is less tender, but I personally prefer it because of its unique, almost gamey, flavor.

Certified organic beef must be fed 100 percent organic feed, although they may also be provided certain vitamin and mineral supplements. Organically raised cattle may not be given hormones to promote growth or antibiotics for any reason. All organically raised cattle must have access to pasture. Organic beef must be certified through the USDA's Agricultural Marketing Service. Cattle must be raised under organic management starting from the last third of gestation. Both grass-finished and grain-fed beef can qualify as organic if they are produced according to organic standards.

According to the USDA, "natural" may be used on the label if the product does not contain any artificial flavors, coloring ingredients, chemical preservatives, or any other artificial or synthetic ingredients. But in fact, almost all beef is natural: **Natural beef** is only minimally processed, but the label does not take into consideration how an animal was raised or what they were fed.

We aren't done yet! Let's talk a little about wet aging versus dry aging. Almost all beef found at the grocery store or in a restaurant has been aged. The aging process allows the naturally occurring enzymes in the beef to break down the muscle tissue, creating more tender and flavorful meat. Today aging is carried out in two ways:

Wet aging is done in Cryovac bags, heavy-duty plastic that holds the meat in its own blood and juices for three to four weeks. The benefit of wet aging to the packer and retailer is that it helps the beef retain its bulk; it loses only about 3 percent of its total weight during the aging process.

Dry aging is done exactly as the name implies; the primal cuts are aged in the open in a cooler that has a controlled temperature and humidity. Ultraviolet lights kill any bad bacteria and promote beneficial ones. Even under the most hygienic conditions, however, the beef forms a moldy crust that must be removed. The benefit of dry aging is that the beef loses moisture, concentrating the beef's flavor, and the bacteria and enzymes develop a deep, rich flavor that can't be matched. The downside is that dry aging results in a 10 to 12 percent weight loss and comes with a high price tag.

Bock-Braised Beef Short Ribs

Beef short ribs have a perfect balance of meat and fat. The meat has a deep, sweet flavor that when slow braised absorbs the cooking liquid; the fat is that perfect gelatinous type that adds a silky mouthfeel to the meat. I like to use Shiner Bock, but you can use your favorite dark beer. This is one of those simple, straightforward recipes that is great for entertaining because you can prepare the ribs ahead. They're also perfect for the weekend because you can pop them in the oven and go about your day. These are great served over green chile grits or some garlicky mashed potatoes.

MAKES 6 SERVINGS

6 pounds short ribs, cut into 1-rib pieces

Kosher salt and freshly ground black pepper

4 tablespoons olive oil

1 large yellow onion, chopped

6 cloves garlic, coarsely chopped

4 carrots, peeled and coarsely chopped

4 stalks celery, coarsely chopped

1 plum tomato, cored and coarsely chopped

2 bay leaves

3 sprigs fresh thyme

1 cup beef demi-glace

1 cup dry red wine

2 cups dark beer

2 tablespoons unsalted butter

2 tablespoons all-purpose flour

2 cups spring onions, diced medium

3 cups button mushrooms, quartered

Preheat your oven to 300°F.

Season the ribs on all sides with salt and pepper. Heat a large Dutch oven over high heat and add 2 tablespoons of the olive oil. Brown the ribs in batches and transfer to a bowl.

Add onion, garlic, carrot, celery, and tomato to the Dutch oven and cook until lightly browned, about 4 minutes. Add the bay leaves, thyme, demi-glace, wine, and beer and bring to a simmer. Add the ribs and any of their juice that has collected in the bowl back to the Dutch oven and return to a simmer. Cover and transfer to the oven. Cook until the meat is tender and beginning to fall off the bone, 2 to 2½ hours.

Transfer the ribs from the braising liquid to a serving dish, cover, and keep warm in a low oven, about 200°F. Strain the braising liquid into a saucepan, discarding the solids. With a ladle, skim off all the fat. Bring to a simmer and reduce the cooking liquid by one-fourth.

Make a quick roux by melting the butter in a small saucepan over medium heat. Whisk in the flour and cook for about 2 minutes. Whisk the roux into the reduced braising liquid and simmer slowly for 5 minutes.

Preheat a large sauté pan over high heat and add the remaining 2 tablespoons of olive oil. Add the onions and mushrooms, lightly season with salt and pepper, and cook until the mushrooms begin to brown, 4 to 5 minutes. Add the mushrooms and onions to the reduced braising liquid, taste for seasoning, and pour over the ribs. Serve immediately.

Salt- and Pepper-Crusted Prime Rib of Beef

As a chef, I'm often asked to name my favorite thing to cook. That's a hard question because my cooking is usually dictated by the season and whomever I'm feeding. If I'm asked what my favorite meal is, however, that's easy: a big slice of prime rib with pan juices and Creamy Horseradish Sauce.

MAKES 6 SERVINGS

1 (6- to 7-pound) bone-in rib roast

1 tablespoon olive oil

¼ cup kosher salt

2 tablespoons freshly ground black pepper

1 tablespoon fresh thyme

2 shallots, finely diced

3 tablespoons all-purpose flour

½ cup dry red wine

2 cups beef stock

Preheat your oven to 325°F.

Coat the roast with the olive oil. In a small bowl, combine the salt, pepper, and thyme. Coat the roast with the salt mixture, pressing it into the meat to form a crust. Place the beef bone side down in a roasting pan. Put the pan in the oven and roast until an instant-read thermometer inserted in the middle of the meat reaches 125°F (for medium rare), 2½ to 3 hours. Remove the roast from the oven and let rest 15 minutes before carving. Meanwhile, make the pan sauce. Pour all but about 3 tablespoons of the fat from the roasting pan. Place the roasting pan on your stove over medium-high heat. Add the shallots and cook until they begin to soften and develop color, about 1 minute. Stir in the flour, scraping any brown bits from the bottom of the pan. Stir in the red wine, again scraping the bottom of the pan. Whisk in the beef stock and bring to a simmer, cooking for about 5 minutes, until thickened.

To serve, cut portions into the desired thickness and spoon pan juices over each slice. Pass the Creamy Horseradish Sauce (page 241).

Smoke-Braised Beef Brisket with Chile-Coffee Rub

We pit braise a lot of different meats at the restaurant. This is a good method for keeping meats that require slow-cooking moist while imparting a smoky flavor to the meat and making a tasty pan sauce at the same time. We use the Chile-Coffee Rub on our traditional pit-smoked beef brisket at the restaurant. The beer and meat drippings marry well with the chile and coffee in the rub to make a great sauce.

MAKES 10 TO 12 SERVINGS

1 beef brisket, 10 to 12 pounds

1 cup Chile-Coffee Rub

3 large carrots, peeled and coarsely chopped

2 yellow onions, coarsely diced

2¹/₄ cups dark beer

Preheat your smoker to 275°F. Rub the brisket all over with the rub and set aside for 30 minutes. Store any leftover rub in an airtight container at room temperature. Arrange the carrots and onions in the bottom of a roasting pan. Pour the beer into the roasting pan with the vegetables. Set the brisket, fat side up, on top of the vegetables. Smoke the brisket until it is tender and shreds easily with a fork, about 8 hours, or 45 minutes per pound to bring the internal temperature to 185°F. Be sure to maintain the smoker temperature between 275°F and 300°F. Remove the meat from the pan and let rest 15 to 30 minutes.

Pour the pan juices and vegetables into a saucepan. Skim the fat from the top of the juices and discard. Slice the meat across the grain and arrange on a platter. Serve the juices and vegetables with the meat.

CHILE-COFFEE RUB

MAKES 2 CUPS

1 cup firmly packed light brown sugar

¹/₂ cup chili powder

2 tablespoons paprika

3 tablespoons kosher salt

2 tablespoons freshly ground black pepper

2 tablespoons finely ground dark-roast coffee

Combine all the ingredients in a mixing bowl and stir to combine well. Store in an airtight container.

I've judged a lot of barbecue contests over the years, and judges always find it hardest to agree on brisket. That's not just because the cooks all have their own special way of barbecuing a brisket, but because the judges always have their own preferences of how they like a brisket to be cooked. The same thing, even more so, applies to you at home—because you are both the cook and the judge.

Here are a few things to consider when you are cooking a brisket:

- Like all meats, quality grade applies to brisket. If you buy a Select grade brisket, the internal marbling will be minimal and your finished meat can be a little dry. I prefer to use a Choice grade brisket and will leave the external fat on the meat during cooking to help keep the brisket moist.

- The proper way to cook a brisket is "low and slow." The optimum temperature to slow smoke is between 275°F and 300°F. Anything higher and you will dry out the meat during the long cooking time. A rule of thumb to follow is to cook a brisket for 45 minutes per pound, or until it reaches an internal temperature of 185°F degrees at its thickest part. Most of the "old timers" still don't use a thermometer when checking to see if their brisket is done. They check it by sticking the brisket with a meat fork and judging how easily the meat separates, or is "fork tender." In the end, it's your brisket and you need to decide how far to cook it—falling apart or firm, or somewhere in the middle.

- Folks have debated for years about the proper seasoning for a brisket. I prefer a simple dry rub of salt, pepper, chile, and brown sugar. The slow smoked brisket will develop a caramelized crust that is perfect in every way. My father is in the "wet mop" camp. He starts the brisket with a dry rub and then will mop the brisket with a thinned down barbecue sauce about every hour during cooking to keep the meat moist.

Maple Sugar- and Mustard-Crusted Rib Eye

The only trick to this recipe is that you have to watch your fire for flare-ups to keep from burning the maple sugar.

MAKES 6 SERVINGS

2 tablespoons olive oil

1/2 cup Dijon mustard

1 tablespoon kosher salt

1 tablespoon freshly ground black pepper

1/4 cup maple sugar

6 rib eye steaks, 10 to 12 ounces each

Start a medium-hot fire in your grill and season the grill grates with a little oil In a small bowl, whisk together the olive oil and mustard. In another bowl, combine the salt, pepper, and maple sugar. Coat both sides of each steak with the mustard mixture and then the maple sugar seasoning. Grill the steaks for about 4 minutes per side for medium-rare. Allow the steaks to rest for 5 minutes before serving.

Mint Pesto Roasted Rack of Lamb

Most folks think of rack of lamb as a special occasion dish you only get in a restaurant. I've never understood this thinking, even more so today, when beautifully frenched racks are so readily available. In the old days, you always saw a little ramekin of mint apple jelly served with lamb chops. This pesto has the mint that many old-timers expect to have with their lamb, but we have given it a little more depth with the addition of garlic, rosemary, and Dijon. This is an easy recipe that you can enjoy on a special occasion, or just make for a quick dinner with the family. Have your butcher french the lamb racks, removing all but a thin layer of fat from the tops of the racks.

MAKES 6 SERVINGS

3 frenched racks of lamb, 14 to 16 ounces each, with 8 bones per rack

2 cups Mint Pesto

Kosher salt and freshly ground black pepper

1/2 cup olive oil

Rub 1 cup of the pesto all over the lamb. Place the racks in a baking pan and cover with plastic wrap. Refrigerate for at least 6 hours, or up to overnight.

Remove the lamb from the refrigerator and allow to come to room temperature, about 30 minutes. Preheat your oven to 450°F.

Place the lamb on a baking rack in a roasting pan and lightly season all over with salt and pepper. Place the roasting pan in the middle of the oven and roast until an instant-read thermometer inserted in the middle reaches 125°F (for medium-rare), 15 to 20 minutes, or it until it reaches your desired degree of doneness. Remove the lamb from the oven and allow to rest on a warm plate tented with foil for 10 minutes before serving.

Transfer the remaining 1 cup pesto to a small mixing bowl and whisk in the olive oil. To serve, cut the lamb into double chops, serving each person two double chops. Drizzle the top of each serving with the pesto.

MINT PESTO

MAKES 2 CUPS

1 cup lightly packed fresh mint leaves

1/4 cup lightly packed fresh basil leaves

2 tablespoons chopped fresh rosemary

6 cloves garlic, coarsely chopped

1/2 cup Dijon mustard

2 tablespoons pecan pieces, lightly toasted

Juice of 1 lemon

1/2 teaspoon kosher salt

1/2 teaspoon freshly ground black pepper

1 cup olive oil

Combine all of the ingredients in a food processor and blend until smooth, about 1 minute. Store in the refrigerator in an airtight container.

Coriander Roasted Leg of Lamb with Border Chimichurri

The earthy flavor of lamb roasted with coriander and garlic pairs perfectly with the bright herbs and sharp red wine vinegar in the chimichurri sauce.

MAKES 6 SERVINGS

4- to 5-pound leg of lamb, butterflied

2 tablespoons olive oil

1 tablespoon freshly ground black pepper

1 tablespoon coriander seeds, toasted and ground

4 cloves garlic, finely chopped

1 tablespoon kosher salt

Border Chimichurri (page 245), for serving

Coat both sides of the lamb with 1 tablespoon of the olive oil. Evenly sprinkle the pepper, coriander, and garlic over both sides of the lamb. Cover with plastic wrap and transfer to the refrigerator, letting the lamb marinate for 2 to 3 hours. About 20 minutes before cooking, remove the lamb from the refrigerator so it can come to room temperature. Preheat your oven to 350°F.

Sprinkle both sides of the lamb with the salt. Heat a large cast-iron skillet or roasting pan over medium-high heat and add the remaining 1 tablespoon of olive oil. Sear the lamb, fat side down, until the surface is dark brown and crispy, 2 to 3 minutes. Turn the lamb over and transfer the skillet to the oven. Cook until an instant-read thermometer inserted in the middle of the lamb reaches 125°F (for medium-rare), 25 to 35 minutes.

Transfer the lamb from the skillet to a platter, loosely tent with foil, and allow it to rest for about 15 minutes before carving (the internal temperature of the lamb will continue to rise). Thinly slice the lamb and serve with the chimichurri.

I WAS FIRST TURNED ON TO CHIMICHURRI by my old running buddy, cowboy cookbook author Grady Spears. We were in Alpine, Texas, in the 1990s when Grady decided that we needed to make a road trip to Ojinaga, Mexico. OJ, as it is known, is a small, dusty border town revered by the young men of West Texas for its beer joints. After an afternoon of sampling beers at the local saloons, Grady dragged me into a hole-in-the-wall "café" on the outskirts of town. We ordered big beef steaks that were served up with hot tortillas, pickled jalapeños, guacamole, and bowls of chimichurri. Their version had a lot of serrano chiles in it to give it a perfect balance of spice and vinegar.

A Guide to Lamb

My father has always loved lamb. One of the first meals I can remember cooking with my father was a slow-roasted leg of lamb studded with garlic and crusted with rosemary and mustard. My brothers, sister, and I always joked that when he was angry with my mother (the daughter of a cattle rancher) he would cook lamb. To this day, whenever I eat lamb, I smile and think of my father.

I have cousins and close friends in the sheep business in the San Angelo area in West Texas. It's almost a spiritual experience for me when I get the chance to visit their ranches. Early summer mornings, when the sheep are grazing in meadows of knee-high dew-covered grass, make you feel like all is right in the world. There is a peace and tranquility to the country, the sheep, and the people who have made a life around sheep ranching. I can understand why sheep were the first domesticated animals and play such a central part in so many cultures and religions.

Ranchers call sheep a dual-purpose animal, bred and raised for both wool and meat production. At the end of World War II there were almost 50 million sheep in the state of Texas alone. Today, there are only about 8 million sheep nationally on about 70,500 ranches and farms. American sheep breeds are larger framed animals than the sheep being raised overseas, producing larger carcasses and higher quality meat. So, for superior size, flavor, and texture, always buy American domestic lamb.

Like beef, all American lamb goes through an inspection by the USDA and is graded according to its quality and yield. There are five grades for lamb, which is always produced from animals that are less than a year old. Normally you will see only two grades in the stores, Prime and Choice. Lower grades of lamb and mutton (meat from sheep over a year old), called Good, Utility, and Cull, are seldom marketed with a quality grade.

Most lamb is fed a combination of mixed grains and grasses, giving the meat a mild flavor that isn't gamey. As demand for quality lamb has grown along with consumers' nutritional concerns, producers are beginning to produce and market grass-finished lamb, certified organic lamb, and all-natural lamb.

Valley Grilled Porterhouse Pork Chops

This has been our best-selling pork dish at the restaurant for years. The brine, best if made from oranges grown in the Rio Grande Valley, is a great way to add flavor and moisture to pork. The combination of the citrus brine with the sweet dry rub, which develops a crust when grilled over an open fire, gives these pork chops a unique flavor.

MAKES 6 SERVINGS

6 (12-ounce) porterhouse pork chops

Citrus Brine

½ cup Brown Sugar Dry Rub (page 96)

Fruited Herb Grain Mustard (page 96), for serving

Place the pork chops in a plastic container or large sealable plastic bag and pour the brine over the chops. Cover or seal the container, place it in the refrigerator, and allow the pork chops to brine for 8 to 12 hours.

Start a medium-hot fire in your grill and season the grill grates with a little oil. Remove the chops from the brine, scrape off any of the spices, and pat dry. Lightly coat each side with the dry rub.

Grill the pork chops until an instant-read thermometer inserted in the middle reaches 165°F, 4 to 5 minutes on each side. Because the chops have a brown sugar rub, watch that your fire does not flare up and that the coals are not too close to the grill grates to help keep the chops from charring.

Transfer the cooked pork chops to a plate and allow them to rest for at least 5 minutes before serving.

CITRUS BRINE

MAKES 4 CUPS

4 cups water

½ cup kosher salt

1 bay leaf

1 teaspoon coriander, toasted

1 teaspoon fennel seeds, toasted

1 teaspoon black peppercorns

¼ cup firmly packed brown sugar

½ cup coarsely chopped yellow onion

2 cloves garlic, crushed

1 orange, quartered

2 sprigs fresh thyme

Bring 1 cup of the water to a simmer and add the salt, bay leaf, coriander, fennel seeds, peppercorns, brown sugar, onion, and garlic. Whisk and simmer until the salt has dissolved, about 1 minute. Add the spice mixture to the remaining 3 cups water. Juice the orange into the brine mixture and add the orange quarters and thyme. Refrigerate until cool.

(continued on next page)

(Valley Grilled Porterhouse Pork Chops, continued)

BROWN SUGAR DRY RUB

MAKES ¹/₂ CUP

¹/₄ cup firmly packed
brown sugar

2 tablespoons kosher
salt

1 tablespoon freshly
ground black pepper

1 tablespoon paprika

1 tablespoon chili
powder

1 tablespoon coriander
seeds, toasted and
ground

1 tablespoon fennel
seeds, toasted and
ground

Combine all of the ingredients in a small mixing bowl. Store in an airtight container.

FRUITED HERB GRAIN MUSTARD

MAKES 2 CUPS

³/₄ cup whole grain
mustard

¹/₂ cup Dijon mustard

³/₄ cup fruit chutney

1 tablespoon finely
chopped chives

1 tablespoon finely
chopped flat-leaf
parsley

¹/₄ teaspoon kosher salt

¹/₂ teaspoon finely
ground black pepper

Combine all the ingredients in a small mixing bowl. Store in the refrigerator in an airtight container.

[A Guide to Pork]

In the 1950s, there were nearly three million pork producers in America. Although that number has dropped to around 67,000 producers today, they are raising more pigs than ever. The family farm that raised pork and a few crops has become a thing of the past. The majority of pork in the United States is produced at big corporate facilities. This has led to the huge growth of the industry and to the United States becoming one of the leading pork producers in the world.

Pork, generally produced from young animals, is not graded with USDA quality grades. That's not a huge concern because the benefit of fewer and larger producers is the uniformity of the size, taste, and tenderness of pork. As with beef and lamb, we are currently seeing a growth in the demand for and production of natural and organic pork.

The key to cooking pork, I think, comes with understanding the best cooking techniques for each cut. Pork is being bred much leaner today, and this lack of fat means that these cuts do not have as much flavor (remember that fat means flavor). To compensate for the relatively small quantity of fat in the prime cuts such as pork loin and chops, make use of brines and marinades to bump up the flavor and add moisture. You also need to be careful that you don't overcook these cuts. Pork ribs and the fatty shoulders and butts are the most tender and flavorful cuts, lending themselves to slow, moist cooking methods such as braising and barbecuing.

Panfried Pork Cutlet with Parsley-Caper Butter Sauce

Texans will batter and fry just about anything and serve it up with a lot of peppery cream gravy. There isn't a café or diner in the state that doesn't offer a chicken-fried steak the size of small child's head. I serve this panfried pork cutlet when I'm trying to be a little fancier than that. It's just as quick and easy as your standard chicken-fried steak, but it shows your guests that you are a bit more serious about your cooking.

MAKES 4 SERVINGS

1¹/₂ pounds pork loin, fat and silverskin removed

¹/₂ cup all-purpose flour

¹/₂ teaspoon kosher salt

¹/₂ teaspoon freshly ground black pepper

1 egg, beaten

¹/₂ cup milk

1 cup bread crumbs, preferably Japanese panko

2 tablespoons unsalted butter

¹/₄ cup olive oil

PARSLEY-CAPER BUTTER SAUCE

1 tablespoon coarsely chopped capers

2 tablespoons white wine

¹/₂ cup cold unsalted butter, cubed

Pinch of kosher salt

Juice of ¹/₂ lemon

2 tablespoons chopped flat-leaf parsley

Cut the pork loin into slices ¹/₂ inch thick. Place the slices between layers of plastic wrap or wax paper and lightly and evenly pound them with a kitchen mallet or heavy skillet, being careful not to tear the meat, to a thickness of about ¹/₈ inch. Combine the flour, salt, and pepper in a pie pan. In a small bowl, whisk together the egg and milk. Spread the bread crumbs in another pie pan. To bread the pork cutlets, lightly dredge each side in the flour mixture, then dip in the egg mixture, and then coat with the bread crumbs.

Heat the butter and olive oil in a large skillet over medium-high heat. In batches, cook the cutlets until golden brown, about 2 minutes per side. Transfer the cutlets to a plate lined with paper towels and hold in a warm oven while you make the sauce.

To make the sauce, discard the oil and wipe out the skillet. Return the pan to medium-high heat and add the capers, stirring to quickly develop a little color, about 1 minute. Add the wine to the pan to stop the capers from cooking and turn the heat to low. The heat of the pan should have reduced the wine to about 1 teaspoon. If all of the wine has evaporated, add a sprinkle of water to moisten the capers. Add the butter a little at a time, slowly whisking as the butter melts to incorporate it with the capers and form a sauce. Season the sauce with the salt, lemon juice, and parsley.

To serve, place a warm cutlet or two on each plate and spoon a little sauce over the top of each.

Slow-Smoked Pork Butt with Vinegar Barbecue Sauce

When I was growing up in West Texas, pork was pretty much limited to bacon and sausage. It wasn't until I was in college and visited friends in Georgia that I discovered my love for pork barbecue—the sweet, smoky meat served with a sharp vinegar barbecue sauce so popular over in the South. This pork butt can be cooked low and slow in a hot smoker, or you can cheat by starting it in your barbecue pit over a slow fire for a couple of hours and then finishing it in your oven.

MAKES 6 SERVINGS

½ cup firmly packed brown sugar

3 tablespoons kosher salt

2 tablespoons finely ground black pepper

3 tablespoons chili powder

2 tablespoons paprika

1 tablespoon garlic powder

5 pounds boneless pork butt

Vinegar Barbecue Sauce (page 251)

Combine the brown sugar, salt, pepper, chili powder, paprika, and garlic power in a mixing bowl and stir to combine. Coat the pork butt with the rub, pressing it into the meat to form a crust.

If using a hot smoker, start your fire and build the temperature to 300°F. Place the pork on the rack with the fat side up. Hot smoke the meat for 6 hours, maintaining the temperature at 275°F to 300°F. After 6 hours, increase to 325°F and continue cooking until the meat is fork-tender and begins to fall apart, about another 2 hours.

If you are using your barbecue pit, start a small fire to one side of the pit. Bring the temperature in the pit to 300°F and place the pork, fat side up, on the opposite side of the pit from the fire. Maintain the temperature in the pit at 300°F by slowly adding more chunks of wood. After about 2 hours, preheat your oven to 300°F. Remove the pork from the pit and wrap in aluminum foil. Place the pork in the oven for 4 hours. Increase the temperature to 325°F and continue cooking until the meat is fork-tender and begins to fall apart, about another 2 hours. Customarily, we serve by putting the pork on a platter so guests can pull off as much as they want. Serve the sauce in a bowl on the side for everyone to slather on as they wish.

Crispy Wild Boar Ribs with Fresh Plum Barbecue Sauce

Wild boar has a mild, sweet wild game flavor that works great with this Asian-inspired plum barbecue sauce. Braising the ribs in apple cider, plum wine, and star anise makes the meat moist and tender while infusing it with great flavor. Finishing the ribs on a hot grill gives them a crispy exterior and a smoky finish. We serve these as an appetizer at Lambert's. When you make them at home, you can substitute baby back pork ribs, if you like.

MAKES 6 SERVINGS

4 pounds wild boar ribs

Salt and freshly ground black pepper

¼ cup olive oil

6 large ripe plums, pitted and coarsely chopped

1 large yellow onion, diced medium

2 carrots, peeled and diced medium

2 stalks celery, diced medium

5 cloves garlic

2 cups apple cider vinegar

2 cups plum wine

½ cup hoisin sauce

½ cup plum jelly

3 whole star anise

1 cinnamon stick

4 green onions, white and green parts, thinly sliced

Preheat your oven to 325°F.

Remove the membrane from the bottom of the ribs and season both sides with salt and pepper. Heat a large roasting pan over high heat and add enough olive oil to coat the bottom of the pan. Sear both sides of the ribs until a deep brown crust develops, 3 to 4 minutes per side. Remove the ribs from the roasting pan. Coat the bottom of the pan with a little more olive oil and add the plums, onion, carrots, celery, and garlic. Cook, stirring occasionally, until the vegetables develop some color, about 5 minutes.

Add the vinegar and plum wine, deglazing the pan, scraping up any brown bits from the bottom of the pan. Stir in the hoisin sauce, jelly, star anise, and cinnamon stick. Add the ribs back to the pan and push down into the liquid and vegetables until partially submerged. Cover the pan with aluminum foil and place in the oven. Cook until the meat is just beginning to pull away from the rib bones, about 2½ to 3 hours. Remove the ribs from the pan and allow to cool in the refrigerator.

To make the plum barbecue sauce, strain the cooking liquid into a medium saucepan, discarding the solids. Bring the liquid to a simmer and reduce until it reaches the thickness of heavy cream, about 15 minutes.

To finish the ribs, start a hot fire in your grill and season the grill grates with a little oil. Cut between the bones for individual ribs and lightly brush with the barbecue sauce. Grill the ribs until nicely charred and heated through, about 3 minutes per side. Toss the char-grilled ribs with ½ cup of the plum barbecue sauce and serve on a platter, drizzling the remaining sauce over the ribs and sprinkling the green onions on top.

[A Guide to Game]

I have hunted deer, antelope, wild boar, and game birds my whole life. We have always followed the "eat what you kill" philosophy of hunting. As a kid, there were quite a few times that our family would sit down to one of my mother's venison dinners only to spend ten minutes trying to chew her attempt at a gourmet meal before ending up in the car, heading to the local drive-in for a burger. By the time I hit my early teens, my father would have the deer processor turn all our yearly kills into ground meat and sausage, because there's no way my mother could make deer chili or breakfast sausage edible.

My mother made the same mistakes that a lot of cooks do when they are cooking game: she forgot that it is much leaner than beef or pork, which makes it easier to overcook until it tastes like shoe leather. My rule of thumb when cooking game is that the only cuts I will grill or pan sear are the tenderloins and loins (chops and loin steaks). The rest either has to be ground for burgers, sausage, and chili or stew meat, or turned into a roast for a slow braise. We've had some cutlets made for frying, which work pretty well, but they can still be a little dry and tough.

Today there are quite a few suppliers of game for both grocers and restaurants. These farm-raised game animals—brought up in large pastures with really high fences—include deer, antelope, elk, moose, bear, buffalo, and wild boar. These animals are not required to undergo USDA inspections or grading standards. Most states, however, offer inspections for the processing of wild game, which are usually killed and processed in the field in mobile, self-contained slaughterhouses. Wild boar (feral hogs), however, fall under the category of "pork" and thus require USDA inspection. At my restaurant, we play it safe and purchase only game that has been inspected by our state agency or out-of-state game that has been inspected by the USDA.

In addition to the Crispy Wild Boar Ribs (page 100) in this chapter, you'll find game recipes throughout this book, including West Texas Venison Chili (page 47), Hunters' Country Venison Pâté (page 62), Sabine Braised Duck with Wild Mushrooms and Port (page 118), Grilled Bacon-Wrapped Quail Stuffed with Chorizo Cornbread (page 121), and Beer-Battered Quail with Jalapeño Peach Glaze (page 122).

POULTRY

TRULY LOVE TO COOK POULTRY, both as a chef, someone who enjoys the process of cooking, and as a student of eating, a fellow who loves to sit down to a good meal. A perfectly roasted plump chicken with tender, moist meat encrusted in a crisp buttery skin, a perfectly grilled quail filled with a spicy stuffing and slathered with a tangy barbecue sauce, or the wild, earthy flavor of a Pecos duck braised with wine, herbs, and mushrooms—that's what I want. Each is cooked using a different method and with different ingredients that bring out the best of the bird.

I could cook and eat a chicken a day for months without repeating the same dish. A chicken is very close to being the chef's perfect meat. The same chicken can be roasted, sautéed, fried, braised, barbecued, poached, or fricasseed, all seasoned only with salt and pepper. Chicken can stand up to a bold curry or rich tomato sauce, be smothered in a country gravy, or be lightly sauced with pan juices that are finished with a little butter and lemon. The key to a great chicken dish is to buy the highest-quality bird available. I don't understand why people will pay up to $20 a pound for a steak to throw on the grill but are reluctant to spend $4 or $5 per pound for an excellent chicken. The quality of a properly raised grain-fed chicken is worth every bit as much as any other meat.

Herbed Chicken and Potato Dumplings

When I think of the memorable foods of my childhood, topping my list is my grandmother's chicken and dumplings—light, airy dumplings with tender chicken and plenty of vegetables in a rich, creamy broth. The dumplings were the magical part of the dish. The closest I could get to the memory of my grandmother's dumplings was by making a variation of Italian gnocchi, a potato dumpling I learned to make while working in San Francisco. The key to these tender potato dumplings is to make them while the potato is still warm and not to overwork the dough.

MAKES 8 SERVINGS

1 whole chicken, 3¹/₂ to 4 pounds

1 tablespoon olive oil

4 carrots, peeled and diced medium

3 stalks celery, diced medium

1 medium yellow onion, diced medium

2 cloves garlic, minced

4 cups chicken stock

2 teaspoons salt

1 teaspoon finely ground black pepper

1 bay leaf

¹/₂ teaspoon dried thyme

Pinch of freshly grated nutmeg

1 cup heavy cream

3 tablespoons unsalted butter

¹/₄ cup all-purpose flour

1 tablespoon finely chopped flat-leaf parsley

1 tablespoon finely chopped chives

DUMPLINGS

1 (1-pound) russet potato

1 tablespoon vegetable shortening

1¹/₂ cups all-purpose flour

1 teaspoon salt

1 teaspoon baking powder

1 egg

Wash and quarter the chicken. Do not go to the trouble of removing the backbone; bones make great stock, and you will be removing the meat from the chicken.

Heat a large soup pot over medium heat and add the olive oil. Add the carrots, celery, and onion to the pot and cook for 3 minutes, stirring occasionally. You want to slowly cook the vegetables to sweat out their flavors. Add the garlic to the vegetables and continue to cook for another 2 minutes. Stack the quartered chicken on top of the vegetables and cover with the chicken stock. If the chicken is not completely submerged in the stock, add a little water to cover it. Season the chicken and stock with the salt, pepper, bay leaf, and thyme and bring to a simmer. Simmer the chicken for 2 minutes and then cover the pot with a lid. Continue to cook the chicken, covered, for another 2 minutes and then turn the heat off from under the pot. Allow the chicken to poach in the hot stock, without removing the lid, for 1 hour.

While the chicken is cooking, make the dumplings. Boil the whole potato in a saucepan with plenty of water until it is cooked through, about 30 to 40 minutes. Remove the skin from the potato and then mash it into a mixing bowl, using a ricer or food mill. If you don't have a ricer or food mill, finely mash with a fork. The trick to a tender potato dumpling is to finely mash the potato without overworking it. Add the vegetable shortening to the warm mashed potatoes and gently fold in to combine.

(continued on next page)

(Herbed Chicken and Potato Dumplings, continued)

In a small bowl, mix together the flour, salt, and baking powder. Add the flour mixture and the egg to the mashed potatoes. With your fingers, gently work the mixture until it comes together into a loose dough. Turn the dough out onto a lightly floured work surface and gently knead until it just comes together into a uniform dough. Cover the dough with a dish towel and let it to rest for 10 minutes. Lightly flour the top of the dough and roll it out to about ¼-inch thick. With a chef's knife, cut the dough into 1½-inch squares. Set aside until the chicken is finished poaching.

Remove the poached chicken from the soup pot to a platter to cool. During the cooking, the chicken should have thrown off a little fat. To remove the fat, skim the surface of the stock with a ladle or large spoon; don't worry about getting every bit, since a little fat left in the stock will add flavor. Add the nutmeg and cream to the pot and bring back to a gentle simmer. Taste the stock and adjust the seasoning, if needed.

Make a quick roux to lightly thicken the stock mixture by melting the butter in a small saucepan over medium heat, stirring in the flour, and cooking for about 2 minutes. Whisk the roux into the stock and gently simmer for 10 minutes.

Once the chicken has cooled to the point that you can handle it, pull all of the meat from the bones, discarding the bones and skin. Next, pull the meat apart into bite-size pieces. Add the chicken meat, parsley, and chives back to the thickened stock.

Add the dumplings to the gently simmering chicken and stock, a few at a time, until the surface of the pot is covered with the dumplings. You may have to push some of the dumplings down into the stock with the back of a spoon to make room for all of the dumplings. Cook the dumplings at a low simmer for 5 minutes with the pot uncovered, then cover the pot and continue to cook for another 5 minutes. Ladle into warm soup bowls to serve.

Panfried Buttermilk Chicken

Marinating chicken in buttermilk both seasons and tenderizes it. Mashed potatoes with plenty of cream gravy and biscuits are almost mandatory to serve alongside the chicken. This is the perfect dish to eat cold at a picnic, or serve it for a summer dinner with a simple garden salad and a cold glass of dry white wine.

MAKES 4 SERVINGS

1 fryer chicken, 3 to 3¹/₂ pounds, cut into 6 pieces (breasts with wings, thighs, and legs)

2 cups buttermilk

1¹/₂ tablespoons kosher salt

¹/₂ teaspoon cayenne pepper

2 cups all-purpose flour

2 teaspoons freshly ground black pepper

2 teaspoons paprika

2 cups vegetable oil

Place the chicken pieces in a bowl or 1-gallon plastic freezer bag. In another bowl, stir together the buttermilk, salt, and cayenne. Pour the marinade over the chicken, turning the pieces to coat them. Cover the bowl or seal the bag and let the chicken marinate in the refrigerator for at least 6 hours, or up to a day.

In a large bowl, whisk together the flour, the remaining 1 tablespoon salt, the black pepper, and paprika. With a pair of tongs, transfer a couple of pieces of chicken at a time from the buttermilk to the flour. Dredge the chicken pieces to generously coat them with the flour before transferring to a platter.

Heat the oil in a large skillet—cast-iron works best—to 360°F. Carefully add the chicken to the oil and fry until golden brown, 10 to 12 minutes. Turn the chicken over and continue to fry until nicely browned, another 10 to 12 minutes. When the chicken is cooked through, an instant-read thermometer inserted into the middle of the pieces should reach 165°F. Transfer the fried chicken to a wire rack or platter lined with paper towels to drain before serving.

VIOLA MOORE, who worked for my grandmother, was famous for her fried chicken and pinto beans. My brothers and I would start begging her at the beginning of the week to fry us some chicken for dinner, and usually by Friday or Saturday Viola would come through. She would cut up the chicken and put it in buttermilk the day before. The next day, when it was time to cook dinner, she would drag out the largest cast-iron skillet I had ever seen. My brothers and I would eagerly watch as she dredged the chicken in seasoned flour and fried it up in hot grease. I miss Viola Moore.

Pan-Seared Rosemary Chicken

When opening the original Lambert's in Austin, I came up with this recipe as our house roast chicken. I still think it's important to roast the chickens to order. I discovered that by splitting them in half and starting them in a searing hot sauté pan, I could reduce the cooking time to about 30 minutes. The chickens come out of the oven with crisp skin and tender, juicy meat. The pan sauce, finished with lemon and butter, is the perfectly simple complement to a perfectly roasted chicken.

MAKES 8 SERVINGS

2 (3 to 3¹/₂-pound) whole chickens

2 tablespoons olive oil

2 tablespoons freshly ground black pepper

2 tablespoons coarsely chopped fresh rosemary

2 tablespoons kosher salt

¹/₄ cup dry white wine

4 tablespoons cold unsalted butter

Juice of 1 lemon

Thoroughly wash the chickens under cold running water and pat the birds dry with paper towels. Remove the chickens' backbones, being careful when cutting around the thighbone not to lose any of the meat. Place the chicken skin side down on your cutting board and split the bird in half by cutting along the breastbone.

Lightly brush or rub both sides of the chickens with the olive oil. Generously season each side of the birds with the pepper and rosemary. Cover and refrigerate until you are ready to cook the chickens, at least 1 hour and up to 1 day.

Preheat your oven to 425°F. Remove the chickens from the refrigerator and season both sides with the salt. Heat a large sauté pan—large enough for 2 chicken halves—over high heat and add just enough oil to coat the bottom of the pan. Carefully place 2 chicken halves, skin side down, in the pan, gently shaking the pan until the chickens start to color and the skin begins to crisp. Allow the chickens to continue cooking, developing a golden-brown crust, about 4 minutes. Turn the chicken over, being careful not to tear the skin, and sear on the meat side for another minute. Remove the chicken from the sauté pan and transfer, skin side up, to a roasting pan large enough to hold all 4 chicken halves. Repeat the process with the remaining 2 chicken halves, adding them to the roasting pan when you are done. Put the pan in the oven and roast until the chicken is golden brown and an instant-read thermometer inserted into the thigh meat reaches 165°F, about 30 minutes. (If I am halving this recipe and cooking only one chicken, I don't bother using a roasting pan; I put the chicken right into the oven in the sauté pan.)

Remove the pan from the oven and transfer the chicken to a platter to rest. Pour off any excess fat from the roasting pan, leaving behind any pan juices and a touch of chicken fat. (Tilt the pan to slowly pour off the top layer of fat, leaving the juices and a little of the chicken fat in the pan.) Place the roasting pan on the stove over medium heat. Add the wine and scrape the bottom of the pan to release any of the browned bits, cooking until the wine is reduced by at least half. Remove the pan from the heat and stir in the cold butter. Finish the pan sauce by stirring in the lemon juice.

To serve the chicken, cut each chicken half into two pieces—the leg and thigh for one piece, and the breast and wing for the other—and return the pieces to the platter. Spoon the lemon-butter sauce over the top of the chicken just before serving.

THE MOST CHALLENGING DISHES TO COOK are usually the ones that seem the simplest and most straightforward. A roasted chicken is a prime example of this. A chicken that is lightly seasoned with salt and pepper, perfectly roasted, and served with a pan jus can be elegant in its simplicity, but since there is no complex sauce or tricky garnish, there's nothing for the chicken to hide behind. My all-time favorite roasted chicken is served at Zuni in San Francisco. Whole chickens are roasted to order in a wood-burning oven, broken down, and served family style. It's nothing fancy, but it still ranks up there among the top ten favorite dishes I've ever eaten.

Wood-Roasted Chicken with Mexican Chocolate Chile Rub

The best way to barbecue a chicken is to hot smoke, or wood roast, the bird over an indirect fire. I have grilled a lot of chickens directly over both wood and coal fires, and invariably the skin burns and tears before the chicken is fully cooked, especially if it has been seasoned with a rub with any sugar in it. The rub on this chicken is a classic combination of brown sugar and chili powder with an undertone of Mexican chocolate. The wood smoke and rub come together to give the chicken a wonderfully unique flavor and crispy skin. Serve this chicken with a bowl of your favorite barbecue sauce.

MAKES 8 SERVINGS

2 (3 to 3½-pound) whole chickens

¼ cup finely grated Mexican chocolate (page 118)

2 tablespoons dark chili powder

2 tablespoons dark brown sugar

2 tablespoons kosher salt

1 tablespoon freshly ground black pepper

1 teaspoon dried oregano

Thoroughly wash the chickens under cold running water and pat the birds dry with paper towels. Remove the chickens' backbones and then split the center of each breastbone with a short whack of your knife—you only want to cut about halfway through the breastbone. Turn the birds over, skin side up, and flatten with the palm of your hand.

To make the spice rub, in a small bowl, stir together the chocolate, chili powder, brown sugar, salt, pepper, and oregano. Generously coat both sides of the chickens with the spice rub. I like to season the chickens with the rub about 30 minutes before I roast them to give the rub a chance to start flavoring the birds; that's about the time it takes to get your fire ready to cook.

Set up your grill or smoker as you would for hot smoking, with the fire to one side of the firebox. Because of the sugar in the rub and the long cooking time, the chickens should not be cooked directly over the live coals. Your fire can be built from charcoal briquettes or wood; either way, let the fire burn until you have a good bed of coals. The grill or smoker should be between 300°F and 325°F. Place the chickens on the grill, skin side up, on the opposite side of the grill from the fire. If I am using charcoal briquettes, I will place a couple of small chunks of hardwood that I have soaked in water on the coals to impart some wood-smoked flavor.

(continued on next page)

(Wood-Roasted Chicken with Mexican Chocolate
Chile Rub, continued)

Roast the chickens until an instant-read thermometer inserted in the middle of the thighs reaches 165°F, about 1 hour, adding charcoal or wood to the fire as needed to keep the temperature at 300°F to 325°F. If you're using a grill, you will need to rotate the chickens a couple of times so that they cook evenly. Once the birds come off the fire, let them rest for at least 15 minutes before carving them into pieces (legs, thighs, wings, and breast halves) and serving.

MEXICAN HOT CHOCOLATE is usually made with bittersweet chocolate that has been mixed with sugar, cinnamon, and milk. It is not as smooth and creamy as American hot chocolate, but has a slightly grainy texture. It is sold under several different brand names in disks containing the chocolate, sugar, and cinnamon.

Sabine Braised Duck with Wild Mushrooms and Port

Braising is a great way to cook both wild and domestic ducks. Most of a duck's fat is found just under the skin, so by first pan searing the duck and crisping the skin, you are rendering off a lot of the fat. The duck's meat, however, is fairly lean, so I like to slowly braise it to keep the meat moist, add flavor, and produce a delicious pan sauce at the same time. I love the earthiness of the mushrooms and the sweetness of the port in this dish, which I usually serve over some buttered egg noodles with a crisp green salad and some crusty bread.

MAKES 4 SERVINGS

1 (5 to 5½-pound) whole duck, quartered and excess fat removed

Kosher salt and freshly ground black pepper

Olive oil for the pan

8 ounces wild mushrooms, such as cremini, shiitake, porcini, chanterelle, or morel, stemmed and halved

6 shallots, peeled and halved

3 cloves garlic, coarsely chopped

¼ cup all-purpose flour

1 cup port wine

2 cups chicken stock

1 bay leaf

1 teaspoon coarsely chopped fresh thyme

2 teaspoons coarsely chopped fresh rosemary

Place a large sauté pan over medium-high heat. As the pan is heating, season both sides of the duck quarters with 2 teaspoons salt and 1 teaspoon pepper. Add enough olive oil to the sauté pan to coat the bottom and add the duck, skin side down. Cook until the skin begins to crisp and turn golden brown, about 8 minutes. Turn the duck over and cook the second side until nicely browned, 6 to 8 minutes more. Transfer the duck, skin side down, to a Dutch oven or deep baking dish.

Preheat your oven to 350°F.

Pour off all but about 3 tablespoons of the fat from the sauté pan into a measuring cup and return the pan to a high heat. When the fat is very hot, add the mushrooms to the pan in a single layer. When the bottoms of the mushrooms begin

to develop color, stir to cook the other side. Lightly season with salt and pepper and transfer the mushrooms to the Dutch oven.

Wipe out the sauté pan, place over medium heat, and add 2 tablespoons of the reserved duck fat from the measuring cup. Add the shallots to the pan and slowly cook until they soften and begin to brown, about 5 minutes. Add the garlic and continue to cook for another 2 minutes. Add another tablespoon of the reserved duck fat to the pan and stir in the flour, cooking for about 2 minutes to make a light roux. Whisk in the port and chicken stock and bring the sauce to a simmer. Season with ¹/₂ teaspoon salt, ¹/₂ teaspoon pepper, the bay leaf, thyme, and rosemary. Pour the liquid over the duck and mushrooms in the Dutch oven. Place on the stove over high heat and bring to a simmer. Cover the Dutch oven and place in the oven. Cook for 45 minutes, then remove from the oven, turn the duck pieces over so that they're skin side up, and return to the oven. Continue cooking until the duck is tender and the meat is just beginning to separate from the bone, about 45 minutes.

Transfer the duck quarters to a warm serving platter. Taste the sauce and adjust the seasoning, if needed. Spoon some of the mushrooms and shallots on top of the duck and pour the remaining sauce into a bowl to pass to your guests at the table.

I FIRST TASTED BRAISED WILD DUCK when my grandmother from Port Arthur was visiting us in Odessa. Some buddies and I had gotten a few ducks on an early morning hunt on the Pecos River. When we showed up at the house with our ducks, my grandmother offered to cook them up for us. I later found out that she had cooked up a lot of ducks for my dad and his buddies when he was my age. My grandmother cut up the ducks and browned the pieces in butter with a lot of onions in a big skillet. She added some Cajun seasonings and milk to the skillet, covered it with a lid, and baked it until the meat just fell off the bones. And, of course, being a good Cajun cook, she served the braised duck with a big pot of white rice.

Grilled Bacon-Wrapped Quail with Chorizo Cornbread Stuffing

It's fairly common practice to wrap quail and dove with bacon before throwing them on a hot grill to keep the lean birds moist during cooking while adding some great bacon flavor. We use a simple brown sugar rub on the birds so we don't overpower the quail meat. The chorizo in the stuffing adds just the right amount of heat and some added fat to keep the birds moist. If you don't have a grill, the quail can be seared on both sides in a hot sauté pan and then finished in a hot oven. Either way, be careful to not overcook the birds; they are best cooked to medium-rare to medium.

MAKES 4 SERVINGS

8 whole semi-boneless quail

Chorizo Cornbread Stuffing (page 122)

2 teaspoons kosher salt

2 teaspoons freshly ground black pepper

2 teaspoons paprika

1 tablespoon brown sugar

8 slices smoked bacon

1$^{1}/_{2}$ cups of your favorite barbecue sauce

2 tablespoons honey

3 tablespoons unsalted butter

Start a hot fire in your grill and season the grill grates with a little oil.

Fill the body cavity of each quail with a large spoonful of the stuffing. In a small bowl, mix together the salt, pepper, paprika, and brown sugar. Dust the outside of each quail with the seasoning mix.

Place the bacon on a cutting board and cover the slices with a layer of plastic wrap. With a meat mallet or the bottom of a small sauté pan, lightly pound the bacon to flatten it out into thinner, wider strips. Wrap the body of each quail with the strips of bacon, securing the ends of the bacon to the quail with a toothpick.

Heat the barbecue sauce to a simmer in a small saucepan. Remove the sauce from the heat and stir in the honey and butter. Separate about $^{1}/_{2}$ cup of the sauce to use for brushing on the quail as it cooks, leaving a little more than 1 cup for serving with the quail.

Grill the quail over a medium-hot fire, turning frequently, until the bacon begins to crisp and the skin has developed nicely browned grill marks, about 10 minutes. Brush both sides of the quail with the barbecue sauce and continue to cook another 2 to 3 minutes. The quail should be cooked to medium rare to medium and the stuffing should just be heated through. Transfer the grilled quail to a warm platter and serve with the remaining barbecue sauce.

(continued on next page)

(Grilled Bacon-Wrapped Quail with Chorizo Cornbread Stuffing, continued)

CHORIZO CORNBREAD STUFFING

MAKES 3 CUPS

8 ounces fresh chorizo sausage, casing removed

¼ cup small-diced yellow onion

3 cloves garlic, minced

1 teaspoon dried sage

Kosher salt and freshly ground black pepper

4 tablespoons unsalted butter

2 cups crumbled cornbread (page 205)

4 green onions, white and green parts, thinly sliced

2 tablespoons chopped cilantro

Chicken stock or water for sprinkling, if needed

Cook the chorizo over medium heat in a large sauté pan. When the chorizo has cooked through and has begun to brown, about 5 minutes, add the onion to the pan and cook until the onion begins to soften, about 2 minutes. Add the garlic and cook for another minute. Season the chorizo with the sage and a sprinkling of salt and pepper.

Remove the pan from the heat and stir in the butter. Add the cornbread, green onions, and cilantro and mix to combine. The fat from the chorizo and the melted butter should provide enough moisture to hold the stuffing together. If the stuffing feels a little dry, sprinkle it with chicken stock or water until it just holds together.

Beer-Battered Quail with Jalapeño Peach Glaze

The only way my mother would cook quail was to panfry them for breakfast and serve them with eggs, biscuits, and pan gravy. The lack of fat in quail, and most game birds, mean that they are easily overcooked. My mother's quick-frying method gave them a crisp coating, and the birds stayed moist. And because I've always loved beer-battered onion rings, we began using the same batter for frying quail at Lambert's. The club soda and beer in the batter produce a light, flavorful crust, too. The Jalapeño Peach Glaze gives the fried quail just the right balance of sweet and sour, with a touch of heat from the chiles.

MAKES 4 SERVINGS

5 semi-boneless quail, quartered

2 tablespoons olive oil

1 teaspoon freshly ground black pepper

1 cup club soda

1 cup dark beer

1¾ cups all-purpose flour

1 teaspoon kosher salt

Pinch of cayenne pepper

Vegetable oil, for frying

1 cup Jalapeño Peach Glaze (page 123)

1 green onion, white and green parts, thinly sliced, for garnish

Arrange the quail quarters on a baking sheet or piece of plastic wrap. Brush both sides of the birds with the olive oil and lightly dust with the black pepper.

Combine the club soda and beer in a large mixing bowl and gradually whisk in the flour. Season the batter with the salt and cayenne. The batter should have the consistency of a thin pancake batter. Allow the batter to rest at room temperature for about 15 minutes before you use it.

To cook the quail, in a large, heavy skillet, heat 3 inches of oil to 360°F. Individually, dip each piece of quail into the batter and then carefully drop into the hot oil. Fry the quail, turning a couple of times, until the batter is golden brown and the meat is just cooked through, 8 to 10 minutes. Transfer the quail to a platter lined with paper towels and hold in a warm oven until all the pieces are fried.

To serve, stack the fried quail on a platter, drizzle with some of the glaze, and sprinkle the green onion on top. Pour the remaining glaze in a bowl for your guests to pass at the table.

JALAPEÑO PEACH GLAZE

MAKES 1¹/₂ CUPS

1 cup white wine

³/₄ cup apple cider vinegar

³/₄ cup peach preserves

3 tablespoons brown sugar

1 teaspoon kosher salt

1-inch piece cinnamon stick

1 tablespoon finely minced fresh ginger

1 tablespoon seeded and finely minced jalapeño

1 green onion, white and green parts, thinly sliced

1 tablespoon chopped cilantro

Combine the white wine, vinegar, peach preserves, brown sugar, salt, cinnamon stick, ginger, and jalapeño in a heavy saucepan and bring to a simmer. Slowly cook the sauce, stirring occasionally, at a low simmer until it has reduced by at least half, 20 to 25 minutes. The sauce will have the consistency of syrup when it is ready. Remove from the heat and stir in the sliced green onion and cilantro. If necessary, the glaze should be gently reheated before spooning over the quail. Any leftover glaze can be cooled and kept in the refrigerator for up to a week.

SEEFOOD

W ALL HAVE FOOD MEMORIES linked to events that centered around food that we remember for the rest of our lives. We look back on those clear recollections of the things we once ate—their taste and their smell—that are linked to the people we were with and the conversations we had.

My mother remembers, as if it were yesterday, going to lunch with her father when she was a small girl. The two of them were eating in the dining room of the Lincoln Hotel in Odessa, which was pretty fancy in its time, with white tablecloths and jacketed waiters. Told she could order anything on the menu, she chose the rainbow trout. She can still describe in detail how the skin was crisp, the meat of the fish was sweet and flaky, and the sauce was buttery, with lemon and parsley. I think the reason this meal has stayed with her for almost seventy years is because it was the first time she ate fresh fish. West Texas in the 1940s was not exactly known for seafood, and fresh fish was pretty much limited to catfish and trout from New Mexico.

My most vivid food memories are related to trips to Port Arthur to visit my grandmother. I recall all the shrimp, oysters, crab, and fish she would cook up for us, because fresh seafood was not the norm for our dinner table when I was growing up. We ate seafood only on special occasions dining out.

Today fresh seafood is available throughout the country, even in Odessa. I can talk to my restaurant's fish guy in Honolulu on Monday to find out what just came in on the boats and have it air freighted to the restaurant by Tuesday. Most large grocers have seafood counters with a variety of fresh fish available year-round. Unfortunately, most folks only think of eating seafood in restaurants. Most of them probably just grew up in a family like mine that didn't cook and eat a lot of seafood at home. Others might be a little intimidated by buying and cooking seafood, but they shouldn't be. Almost anything that you can do with chicken, beef, or pork, you can do with seafood.

Fire up the barbecue grill, because you can treat a meaty piece of tuna, swordfish, or snapper just like a steak. Simply season the fish with salt and pepper, or get imaginative with a marinade or dry rub. I love to crust a grilled tuna steak with cracked pepper and ginger and serve it with a sweet teriyaki sauce. Swordfish is perfect grilled with an ancho-brown sugar dry rub and a spicy barbecue sauce. Redfish grilled with Cajun seasoning and served with Creole shrimp would do my grandmother proud. Because fish doesn't have internal marbling like beef, you need to grill it over a hot fire to get a good crust and grill marks, and quickly cook it through. Don't overcook your fish to ensure that the meat stays moist and tender.

If you can fry bacon in a skillet, you can sauté a piece of fish. Firmer varieties like halibut, redfish, and salmon can be seasoned and go directly into a hot sauté pan. You'll want to use a very hot pan that has been coated with fat; the fat should be rippling and have just begun to smoke when you add the fish. This will keep the fish from sticking and help it develop a good crust, which adds flavor and helps seal in the fish's moisture. When cooking thicker pieces of fish, like a big fillet of bass, I usually get a good crust on the first side, flip the fish over, and finish the fish in a hot oven for a few minutes. When I'm sautéing a more delicate fish like sole, I'll usually lightly dust the fillet with flour, which will help the fish hold together and develop a crust.

A quality piece of fresh fish that has been properly cooked can be served with nothing more than a wedge of lemon. Or you can get creative like me, a chef who loves to pair sauces with food. A quick mayonnaise-based tartar sauce goes with almost any fish; try the Serrano-Lime Tartar Sauce with the Seafood Fritto Misto (page 132) to see what I mean. I think a vinegar-based salsa or relish works great with a fatty fish like a salmon or tuna, like the Mint-Cucumber Relish (page 147) or the Fennel Salsa Verde (page 246). Or you can go old-school with a hollandaise sauce, or even a little bolder with a barbecue or chile sauce. A sautéed fish is usually finished with a quick pan sauce. After the fish is cooked, it's transferred to a serving plate and the same pan is used for the sauce. Butter can be lightly browned and finished with parsley and lemon juice for a meunière sauce. Add shallots, white wine, and vinegar, reduce the sauce, and finish it with cold butter for a simple beurre blanc. Sauté some garlic, red pepper flakes, anchovy, and tomato to take any sautéed fish over the top.

Get to know the guy or gal at your local fish market on a first-name basis; Jim's my guy at Central Market. They can let you know what's really fresh and what they have coming in during the week each season. If they don't have what you are looking for, they can probably order it. Jim ordered me some amazing fresh anchovies not long ago.

So fire up the grill or heat up the skillet and start cooking seafood. It's the only way you will learn how to do it and find out what your favorite seafood is. Get a few seafood dishes into your repertoire of the foods that you love to cook, and create some food memories for your family and friends.

[Oysters and "R" Months]

When I was growing up, people would say that you shouldn't eat raw oysters in months that don't have an "R" in them—in other words, the summer months. Some people still say it, but this old wives' tale is just a myth. Oysters on the half shell are safe to eat year round. The R-month dictate was probably started before refrigeration was widely available, and highly perishable oysters would quickly spoil in the heat of the summer. Actually, oysters are at their peak of plumpness in May and June. They start the spawning season in July and August, when they can be a little soft and milky, but they are still safe to eat.

Always buy your oysters fresh and store them in the refrigerator over ice in a perforated pan that allows for drainage, covered with a damp towel. Fresh oysters will keep about a week in the refrigerator but are best eaten within a couple of days. Preshucked oysters work great for recipes like gumbo. They should come covered with liquid in a sealed container. Shucked oysters in their liquor freeze well for up to 3 months and are fine for use in cooked soups and stews.

Broiled Oysters with Spinach, Bacon, and Pernod

Over the years we've cooked a lot of oysters on the half shell, grilling them with bacon and barbecue sauce, topping them with a creamy sweet potato puree, or broiling them with roasted tomatoes and peppers. The original baked oyster dish was oysters Rockefeller, served at Antoine's in New Orleans. My favorite has always been oysters broiled with spinach, bacon, and Pernod. It's a nod to the classic Rockefeller with the addition of bacon, cream, and Parmesan.

MAKES 6 SERVINGS

1 tablespoon olive oil

2 slices bacon, finely diced

2 shallots, finely diced

3 cloves garlic, minced

1/2 teaspoon red pepper flakes

1 teaspoon coarsely chopped fresh thyme, or 1/2 teaspoon dried thyme

6 ounces fresh spinach, stemmed

Kosher salt and freshly ground black pepper

1/2 cup heavy cream

2 tablespoons Pernod

3/4 cup finely grated Parmesan cheese

Rock salt for the baking sheet

24 fresh oysters

1 lemon, cut into 6 wedges

To make the spinach topping, heat a large, heavy sauté pan over medium-high heat and add the olive oil. Add the bacon and cook until it begins rendering its fat and starts becoming crisp, about 4 minutes. Add the shallots and cook until soft, about 1 minute more. Stir in the garlic, red pepper flakes, and thyme. Add the spinach to the pan (if the pan seems too full, don't worry; it will quickly cook down) and, using a pair of tongs, continually fold the spinach from the bottom of the pan to the top, until it is all wilted. Lightly season with salt and pepper.

Transfer the spinach mixture from the sauté pan to a colander. With the back of a large, heavy spoon, press the mixture into the colander to remove as much moisture as possible. Place the spinach mixture on a cutting board and finely chop with a chef's knife. Transfer to a mixing bowl.

Combine the cream and Pernod in a small saucepan and bring to a simmer. Cook until reduced by half and add to the spinach mixture. Add 1/4 cup of the Parmesan and stir to combine. Refrigerate while you shuck the oysters.

Preheat the broiler.

Cover the bottom of a large baking sheet with about 1/4 inch of rock salt. Shuck each oyster and arrange on the rock salt in the bottom half of their shell. Top each oyster with a generous tablespoon of the spinach mixture. Sprinkle the remaining 1/2 cup Parmesan on the top of the oysters. Place under the broiler until the oysters begin to bubble and the topping is nicely browned, about 8 minutes. Divide the oysters among 6 serving plates and garnish each plate with a lemon wedge before serving.

Mexican Ceviche Cocktail

Seafood makes a perfect appetizer or a light summer dinner. To make ceviche at the restaurant, we use shrimp and a firm, white-flesh fish—such as drum, snapper, or halibut—that has been lightly poached and then tossed with a lot of citrus and pico de gallo. Bay scallops and lump crabmeat also make great additions to a ceviche.

MAKES 6 SERVINGS

8 cups water

3 tablespoons kosher salt

1 tablespoon red pepper flakes

2 bay leaves

Juice of 2 lemons

1 pound medium shrimp, peeled and deveined

1/2 pound firm whitefish, cut into 1-inch pieces

Juice of 3 to 4 limes

Kosher salt and freshly ground black pepper

3 plum tomatoes, cored and diced small

1 ripe avocado, pitted, peeled, and diced small

1 serrano chile, seeded and finely chopped

5 green onions, white and green parts, finely chopped

1/2 cup finely diced red onion

1/2 cup finely chopped cilantro

2 cups shredded iceberg or romaine lettuce

Tortilla chips, for serving

Combine the water, salt, red pepper flakes, bay leaves, and lemon juice in a saucepan and bring to a simmer over high heat. Add the shrimp and fish to the liquid and turn the heat down to maintain a slow simmer. Poach the seafood until it is just cooked through, about 2 minutes. Gently remove the seafood from the liquid with a strainer and transfer to a large baking sheet, shaking the pan until the seafood forms a single layer. Squeeze the juice of one lime over the top of the seafood and lightly season with kosher salt. Place the baking sheet with the seafood in the refrigerator to cool for about 30 minutes.

Transfer the chilled seafood to a large mixing bowl. Add the tomatoes, avocado, serrano chile, green and red onions, and cilantro. Squeeze two more limes over the mixture and lightly season with salt and pepper, gently stirring to combine. Taste the ceviche and adjust seasoning with more lime juice and salt and pepper, if needed.

To serve, make bed of shredded lettuce in the bottom of chilled glass bowls and top each with a large scoop of ceviche. Serve with plenty of freshly fried tortilla chips.

Seafood Frito Misto

This dish reminds me of vacations to the coast in Mexico. We'd sit at a small beach restaurant, drink cold margaritas, and devour platters of freshly caught shrimp, fish, and squid that had been lightly fried with flour and corn masa. Don't be afraid to change up the seafood in this recipe; add some scallops, oysters, or even onions and green beans to the mix.

MAKES 4 SERVINGS

12 large shrimp, peeled (but with the tail left on), deveined, and butterflied

1/2 pound sole fillets, cut into 1 by 3-inch strips

1/2 pound squid, cleaned, bodies cut into 1/2-inch rings, tentacles left whole

1 cup buttermilk

2 cups all-purpose flour

1/2 cup corn masa or cornmeal

Kosher salt and freshly ground black pepper

4 cups vegetable oil

Serrano-Lime Tartar Sauce, for serving

Rustic Chile Pepper Sauce (page 249), or store-bought chili sauce, for serving

4 limes, cut into wedges, for serving

Place the shrimp, sole, and squid in three separate bowls. Add one-third of the buttermilk to each bowl and lightly toss to coat the seafood.

In a large mixing bowl, stir together the flour, masa, 2 teaspoons salt, and 2 teaspoons pepper.

Add the oil to a large Dutch oven and heat to 375°F. Preheat the oven to 200°F. Fry the seafood in batches, starting with the shrimp. Place the shrimp in a wire strainer basket and shake off any excess buttermilk. Toss the shrimp in the seasoned flour to coat and then carefully drop into the hot oil. Fry the shrimp until they just begin to develop color and are cooked through, about 4 minutes. Place the fried shrimp on a platter lined with paper towels, lightly sprinkle with salt, and transfer to the oven to keep warm while you fry the remaining seafood. Repeat the process with the sole and squid, tossing them in the seasoned flour, frying in the hot oil, and sprinkling with salt. Serve the fried seafood with the tartar sauce, chili sauce, and lime wedges on the side.

SERRANO-LIME TARTAR SAUCE

MAKES ABOUT 1 1/2 CUPS

1 cup good-quality mayonnaise

1 small serrano chile, seeded and finely diced

1 clove garlic, minced

1 tablespoon finely diced white onion

1 tablespoon chopped cilantro

1 teaspoon chopped capers

Juice of 1 lime

Kosher salt and freshly ground black pepper

Combine all the ingredients in a mixing bowl, using a bit less of the serrano chile if you'd prefer a less spicy sauce. The sauce can be stored in the refrigerator in an airtight container for several days.

Scampied Barbecued Shrimp

My Uncle Francis used to take us to a restaurant in Sabine Pass that was famous for its barbecued crab and cold beer. The barbecued crab was actually not barbecued at all, but instead cooked with barbecue seasoning and served with a lot of melted butter. I borrowed their idea and started doing the same thing with shrimp when we opened the first Lambert's in Austin.

MAKES 6 TO 8 SERVINGS

1½ pounds large shrimp, peeled and deveined

Kosher salt and freshly ground black pepper

2 tablespoons olive oil

5 cloves garlic, finely chopped

¼ cup white wine

1 cup Lambert's Barbecue Sauce

Juice of 1 lemon

4 tablespoons cold unsalted butter, cubed

1 tablespoon chopped flat-leaf parsley

1 tablespoon thinly sliced green onion, white and green parts

6 to 8 thick slices of garlic cheese bread, for serving

Lightly season the shrimp on both sides with salt and pepper. Heat a large sauté pan over high heat and add the olive oil. Place the shrimp in the pan in a single layer (you might have to cook the shrimp in two batches). As soon as the shrimp begin to develop color, about 2 minutes, turn the shrimp over and add the garlic. Continue cooking the shrimp for another 2 minutes and then stir to allow all of the garlic to come in contact with the pan.

As soon as the garlic starts to develop color, add the wine to the pan and cook until it is reduced by half, about 1 minute. Stir in the barbecue sauce and bring to a simmer. Add the lemon juice and remove the pan from the heat. Stir in the butter and parsley until the butter is completely incorporated.

Ladle the shrimp and sauce onto plates and garnish with the green onion. Serve with thick slices of garlic cheese bread.

LAMBERT'S BARBECUE SAUCE

MAKES 4 CUPS

2 tablespoons olive oil

1 small yellow onion, finely diced

3 cloves garlic, minced

¼ cup firmly packed brown sugar

3 tablespoons chili powder

1 tablespoon paprika

2 tablespoons freshly ground black pepper

1 tablespoon kosher salt

1 teaspoon dried oregano

½ cup apple cider vinegar

¼ cup Dijon mustard

2½ cups ketchup

Heat a saucepan over high heat and add the olive oil. Add the onion and garlic and sauté until the onion is soft and the garlic has begun to develop a bit of color, 2 to 3 minutes.

Add the brown sugar, chili powder, paprika, pepper, salt, and oregano, stirring to coat the onion mixture. Add the vinegar, mustard, and ketchup, bring to a simmer, and turn the heat down to low. Cook at a low simmer for 10 minutes to blend the flavors. Let the sauce cool and store, covered, in the refrigerator.

IF YOU DON'T HAVE TIME TO MAKE THE BARBECUE SAUCE I use here, you can just use your favorite barbecue sauce in this recipe instead. Finishing the sauce with butter makes the dish deliciously rich, but be careful not to allow the sauce to come to a boil once the butter has been added, as it can cause the butter to separate out.

Shrimp Rigatoni Puttanesca

In Lambert's version of pasta puttanesca, the classic Italian tomato sauce with olives, capers, and anchovies, we start the sauce with chorizo sausage to add a little more depth of flavor, and then we finish it with some heavy cream for richness. The pan-seared shrimp are the finishing touch to a perfect pasta. A rich, creamy sauce calls for a big pasta like a rigatoni that will stand up to and hold a lot of the sauce.

MAKES 6 SERVINGS

1 pound rigatoni

6 tablespoons olive oil, divided use

4 ounces fresh chorizo sausage, casing removed

1 shallot, finely diced

6 cloves garlic, finely diced

1/2 teaspoon red pepper flakes

6 anchovy fillets, finely chopped

2 tablespoons capers, coarsely chopped

1/2 cup kalamata olives, pitted and coarsely chopped

1/2 cup white wine

1 (28-ounce) can Italian diced tomatoes, drained

Kosher salt and freshly ground black pepper

2 teaspoons sugar

1/4 cup coarsely chopped, loosely packed fresh basil

1 cup heavy cream

1 pound medium shrimp, peeled and deveined

1 teaspoon paprika

1/4 cup freshly grated Parmesan cheese

Bring a large pot of salted water to a boil. Add the pasta and cook until al dente, about 12 minutes or according to the package directions. Drain the pasta and transfer to a large bowl. Toss the pasta with 1 tablespoon of the olive oil and keep warm while you're finishing the sauce and shrimp. Cover, and hold at room temperature.

While the pasta is cooking, start the sauce. Heat a large saucepan over medium-high heat and add 3 tablespoons of the olive oil. Add the chorizo and cook until it begins to brown and crumble, about 4 minutes. Add the shallot, garlic, and red pepper flakes to the pan and cook for 1 minute. Add the anchovy, capers, and olives and continue to cook for another minute. Add the white wine and deglaze the pan, scraping up any brown bits from the bottom. Cook until the wine is reduced by half, then stir in the tomatoes, salt, pepper, sugar, basil, and cream. Bring the sauce to a simmer and cook, stirring frequently, until the sauce thickens slightly, about 10 minutes.

While the sauce is simmering, cook the shrimp. Season both sides of the shrimp with salt, pepper, and paprika. Heat a large skillet over high heat and add the remaining olive oil. Add the shrimp to the skillet in a single layer and sear the first side until a crust forms on the bottom, about 2 minutes. Turn the shrimp and sear the second side until the shrimp are cooked through, about 2 minutes more. Transfer the shrimp to a warm plate.

To serve, add the pasta to the hot puttanesca sauce and toss to combine. Divide the pasta among your serving plates and top each plate with an equal amount of the sautéed shrimp. Sprinkle the Parmesan on top and serve immediately.

Redfish with Shrimp Creole

The perfect topping for a pan-seared redfish is Shrimp Creole, sweet Gulf shrimp swimming in a peppery tomato sauce. Sometimes I double the batch of Shrimp Creole, saving some to serve the next day over a big bowl of white rice. Serve this dish plenty of white rice, crusty bread, and bottles of Louisiana hot sauce.

MAKES 4 SERVINGS

4 (6-ounce) redfish fillets, $1/2$- to $3/4$-inch thick each

2 teaspoons kosher salt

1 teaspoon freshly ground black pepper

$1/2$ teaspoon white pepper

Pinch of cayenne pepper

2 teaspoons paprika

1 teaspoon Old Bay Seasoning

$1/4$ teaspoon dried thyme

$1/4$ teaspoon dried oregano

Olive oil for the pan

Shrimp Creole

Arrange the fish fillets in a single layer on a platter. In a small bowl, stir together the salt, black and white pepper, cayenne, paprika, Old Bay Seasoning, thyme, and oregano. Generously dust both sides of the fish with the seasoning mixture, gently pressing it into the fish with your fingers.

Heat a large skillet over high heat and add enough olive oil to coat the bottom of the pan. As soon as the oil just begins to smoke, carefully add the fish to the pan. Gently shake the pan to help keep the fish from sticking. Sear the fish until it develops a deep brown color, 3 to 4 minutes. Turn the fish over with a metal spatula and continue cooking until cooked through, another 3 to 4 minutes.

Transfer the fish to warmed serving plates and top with a big ladleful of the Shrimp Creole.

SHRIMP CREOLE

MAKES 4 SERVINGS

$1^1/2$ pounds medium shrimp

$1/4$ cup vegetable oil

$1/4$ cup all-purpose flour

1 cup small-diced yellow onion

1 cup small-diced celery

1 large small-diced green bell pepper

$1/2$ cup thinly sliced green onions, white and green parts

2 cloves garlic, finely chopped

1 teaspoon salt

1 teaspoon sugar

1 teaspoon freshly ground black pepper

Pinch of cayenne pepper

$1/4$ teaspoon dried thyme

2 bay leaves

1 (14.5-ounce) can diced tomatoes, with their liquid

1 (8-ounce) can tomato sauce

2 tablespoon tomato paste

1 cup shrimp or chicken stock

2 tablespoons chopped flat-leaf parsley

Peel and devein the shrimp, reserving the shrimp shells for a shrimp stock, and set aside.

Heat a large saucepan or Dutch oven over medium heat and add the vegetable oil and flour to make a roux. Cook the roux, stirring, until it develops a golden color, 15 to 20 minutes. Stir in the onion, celery, bell pepper, and green onions and cook until the vegetables begin to soften, about 5 minutes. Add the garlic, salt, sugar, pepper, cayenne, thyme, and bay leaves and cook for another 1 minute. Add the diced tomatoes with their liquid, the tomato sauce and paste, and shrimp stock and stir to combine. Bring to a boil, reduce the heat to a simmer, and cook for 30 minutes, stirring occasionally.

Add the shrimp and cook until they curl and turn pink, about 5 minutes. Stir in the parsley and serve while still warm.

WHENEVER MY FATHER DISAPPEARS FOR A FEW DAYS, chances are he's on the Texas coast fishing with his buddies. If I'm lucky, he'll let me disappear with him. We pretty much stick to bay fishing for trout, flounder, black drum, and, of course, Gulf redfish. Bay fishermen love to catch reds, both for the sport and the eating. Redfish have firm white meat that can stand up to almost any preparation or seasoning. I love to season the fillets with a spicy Cajun dry rub and cook them on a smoking hot grill or skillet.

Panfried Trout with Crab and Shrimp Stuffing

Panfrying is my favorite way to cook and eat a trout; it crisps the skin while keeping the meat flaky and moist. This sweet seafood stuffing of crab and shrimp puts the trout over the top. If you don't want to serve the fish with a creamy tartar sauce, try a simple butter sauce or just a few wedges of lemon.

MAKES 4 SERVINGS

4 (10-ounce) whole trout, cleaned and heads removed

STUFFING

2 tablespoons unsalted butter

1/4 cup finely diced white onion

1 stalk celery, finely diced

1/2 cup bread crumbs, preferably Japanese panko

12 medium shrimp, peeled, deveined, poached, and halved lengthwise

4 ounces crabmeat, picked over for bits of shell

2 tablespoons mayonnaise

1 teaspoon fresh lemon juice

2 tablespoons chopped flat-leaf parsley

Kosher salt and freshly ground black pepper

FRY COATING

1 cup all-purpose flour

1/2 cup cornmeal

1 teaspoon kosher salt

1 teaspoon freshly ground black pepper

2 cups vegetable oil

1 lemon, quartered, for garnish

Serrano-Lime Tartar Sauce, (page 132), for serving

Rinse the trout under cold running water and pat dry with paper towels. Set aside.

To make the stuffing, heat a sauté pan over medium-high heat and add the butter. When the butter is melted, add the onion and celery and sauté until soft, about 3 minutes. Transfer to a mixing bowl and allow to a cool for a few minutes. Add the bread crumbs, shrimp, crab, mayonnaise, lemon juice, and parsley and lightly season with salt and pepper. Stir to combine, taste the stuffing, and adjust the seasoning, if needed.

Evenly fill the cavity of each trout with the stuffing. To help hold the stuffing in place, pull the two sides of the fish together and secure with a toothpick.

In a shallow pan or pie dish, stir together the flour, cornmeal, salt, and pepper. In a large, heavy skillet, heat the oil to 375°F. Dredge each trout in the flour mixture, generously coating both sides of the fish. Fry the trout on the first side until it is brown and crispy, 4 to 6 minutes. Turn the trout over and fry the other side for another 4 to 6 minutes. Transfer to a platter lined with paper towels. Serve the trout immediately with the lemon wedges and tartar sauce.

GORDON HEADLEE, one of my mother's childhood friends and a neighbor rancher, got tired of the wind and heat of West Texas and bought a ranch outside Gunnison, Colorado, when I was a teenager. Gordon loved the cattle business, but I think he loved to fish for trout more. I spent a lot of summers fly-fishing for trout with Gordon on the streams and rivers around Gunnison. Although I got to be a pretty good fly fisherman, I think I'm better at cooking trout than catching them.

Romesco-Crusted Snapper with Basil Beurre Blanc

I learned to make romesco sauce when I worked at Postrio in San Francisco, where I fell in love with its complex purity. I think of romesco as a red pepper and tomato pesto, with a mix of garlic, nuts, Parmesan, and olive oil. Romesco works wonderfully with seafood and is the perfect topping for meaty, boldly flavored snapper. A classic beurre blanc seasoned with fresh basil is a great complement to the garlicky romesco.

MAKES 4 SERVINGS

2 tomatoes, cored and halved

¼ cup medium-diced white onion

4 cloves garlic

¼ cup olive oil

Kosher salt and freshly ground black pepper

¼ teaspoon red pepper flakes (optional)

1 tablespoon paprika

¼ cup sliced almonds, toasted

1 red bell pepper, roasted, peeled, seeded, and coarsely chopped

2 tablespoons chopped fresh basil

2 tablespoons freshly grated Parmesan cheese

1 tablespoon red wine vinegar

4 (6-ounce) skinless red snapper fillets

Basil Beurre Blanc (page 143)

6 fresh basil leaves, thinly sliced, for garnish

Preheat your oven to 350°F.

To make the romesco sauce, line a baking sheet with a piece of aluminum foil and arrange the tomato halves (cut side up), onion, and garlic on top (roasted tomatoes can stick to the baking sheet, and the foil makes cleanup a lot easier). Drizzle with 1 tablespoon of the olive oil and lightly season with salt, pepper, and red pepper flakes. Roast in the oven until the tomatoes begin to collapse and the onion and garlic are soft, about 30 minutes.

Place the roasted vegetables in your food processor or blender and add the paprika, almonds, bell pepper, basil, Parmesan, vinegar, and remaining olive oil. Pulse the machine 4 or 5 times, until all the ingredients come together into a coarse paste. Taste and adjust the seasoning, if needed. Transfer the romesco sauce to a covered container and store in the refrigerator until you are ready to cook the fish. Make up to 1 day in advance.

Preheat your oven to 400°F.

Lightly oil a baking sheet (you can use the same one you used to roast the vegetables, without the foil). Arrange the snapper fillets on the baking sheet and lightly season with salt and pepper. Top each fillet with a large spoonful of the romesco. Evenly spread the romesco to about ¼-inch thickness. Roast the fish in the middle of the oven until the romesco begins to turn crusty and brown and the fish is cooked through, 12 to 15 minutes.

To serve, transfer the fish to serving plates with a large metal spatula. Place a spoonful of the beurre blanc beside the fish and garnish the fish with the basil. Serve immediately.

BASIL BEURRE BLANC

MAKES ³/₄ CUP

½ cup loosely packed
fresh basil leaves

¼ cup heavy cream

¼ cup white wine

1 tablespoon white wine
vinegar

1 shallot, finely chopped

½ teaspoon black
peppercorns

½ cup cold unsalted
butter, cubed

Kosher salt

1 teaspoon fresh lemon
juice

Combine the basil and cream in a blender and puree until smooth. Set aside.

In a small saucepan, bring the white wine, vinegar, shallot, and black peppercorns to a simmer. Cook until the liquid is reduced to ¼ of its original volume, 5 to 10 minutes. Add the basil-cream puree and return to a simmer for about a minute.

Remove the pan from the heat and whisk in the cold butter, one cube at a time, whisking continually until thoroughly incorporated. Strain the sauce into a bowl, discarding the solids, and season the sauce with salt and the lemon juice. Keep the beurre blanc warm until you're ready to serve, transfer to a small bowl, place it in a larger bowl of warm water, and cover.

[Purchasing Fresh Fish]

When purchasing fish for the restaurant, we try to always buy them whole and then break them down into individual portions ourselves. When buying fish whole, it's easier to judge its freshness by looking for clear eyes, firm flesh, bright red gills, and clean, shiny skin. We have skilled cooks, though, who can properly break down the fish.

Most home cooks don't know how to break down whole fish, so it's fine to buy fillets. Find the market in your area that sells the most fresh fish; this usually means that they are turning over their inventory, ensuring you are getting the freshest fish. The fillets should be shiny and firm to the touch, never dull, slimy, or with a fishy smell. If it's not fresh, don't buy it. Once you get the fish home, it's best eaten within one or two days. Remember that your fresh fish has already been out of the water for several days between the boat and the grocery store.

If you can't buy good fresh fish, the next best thing is frozen. Most big commercial fishermen freeze their catch hours after it comes out of the water. You can't get much fresher than that. The downside to frozen fish is that the freezing process expands the moisture in the fish, causing expansion in the cells, which can cause the texture of the fish to be a little soft. This is not a big problem with firm, meaty fish like tuna, cod, and halibut, but it can cause more delicate fish, like sole and flounder, to become a little mushy when cooked. I'll often freeze fresh fish from the market or a fishing trip when I know I won't eat it within a day or two. Wrap it well with a heavy butcher paper and it will hold in the freezer for up to 3 months.

Roasted Halibut in Saffron Tomato Broth with Corn Fritter Dumplings

I remember a café in Georgia that served bowls of braised greens with corn dumplings. I tried serving similar corn dumplings and sautéed chard with fish and it turned out great. This is one of those dishes that reminds me that food with humble ingredients is often the best.

MAKES 4 SERVINGS

4 (6-ounce) halibut fillets, about 1½ inches thick each

Olive oil

Kosher salt and freshly ground black pepper

2 tablespoons julienned fresh basil

1 shallot, cut into ⅛-inch julienne

12 cherry tomatoes

4 cups Swiss chard, turnip greens, or mustard greens, stemmed and cut into 2-inch strips

2½ cups Saffron Tomato Broth (page 146)

Squeeze of fresh lemon juice

16 Corn Fritter Dumplings (page 146)

Preheat your oven to 375°F.

Season the halibut fillets by very lightly coating the top of each fillet with olive oil and a sprinkling of salt and pepper. Divide 1 tablespoon of the basil among the 4 fillets. Heat a large skillet over high heat and add enough olive oil to coat the bottom of the pan. Place the halibut fillets in the hot skillet, seasoned side down, and gently shake the pan to keep the fish from sticking. Cook the fish until a nice brown crust develops, about 3 minutes. Turn the fish over and place the skillet in the oven to finish cooking, about 5 minutes.

While the fish is cooking, heat a sauté pan over high heat and add 1 tablespoon olive oil. Add the shallot and cook until it softens and begins to color, about 2 minutes. Add the cherry tomatoes and chard to the pan and lightly season with salt and pepper. Sauté until the chard just begins to wilt, about 1 minute. Add ¼ cup of the Saffron Tomato Broth and cook until the broth has reduced by half and the chard is cooked through, another 2 minutes. Set aside and keep warm until ready to serve.

In a large saucepan, heat the remaining 2¼ cups of the Saffron Tomato Broth to a simmer and add the lemon juice. Taste and adjust the seasoning, if needed. Add the dumplings to the saucepan, cover, and allow them to heat through, about 2 minutes.

To serve, arrange a halibut fillet in the middle of a wide soup bowl. Spoon 3 of the cherry tomatoes and some of the chard around each piece of fish. Arrange 4 dumplings on each plate. Ladle ½ cup of broth over each piece of halibut and garnish with the remaining basil.

(continued on next page)

TEX-MEX

WHEN FRIENDS ARRIVE IN TEXAS from either the East or West coast, the first thing they ask is to be taken to a Mexican restaurant. I've lived in New York and San Francisco, so I know firsthand how it feels to be deprived of a proper plate of Mexican food. San Francisco might have the Mission district, where you can find some pretty decent burritos, but it doesn't come close to a No. 1 combination plate: cheese enchiladas smothered with a chili gravy, a smoky barbacoa taco, tamales, Spanish rice, and refried beans. That's Tex-Mex food, and I crave it at least twice a week.

Tex-Mex cuisine got its start back when Texas was a part of the Northern Frontier of Mexico. Anglo settlers and Tejanos (Texans of Mexican descent) melded their cooking styles and food preferences with those of the native Mexican Indians and Spaniards. As Texas evolved, so did Tex-Mex cuisine. With its roots in south Texas ranching country, Tex-Mex spread throughout Texas and eventually the United States.

Many people think that Tex-Mex is Mexican food, or what people in Mexico eat. Some ingredients and cooking methods might be shared by Tex-Mex and Mexican cuisines—the use of chiles, masa, rice, beans, and certain spices, for example, or the fondness for throwing things on the grill. But there are also a lot of ingredients unique to Tex-Mex, like melted yellow cheese and cumin, as well as dishes that you will only find in Texas, like chili con queso, chili gravy, nachos, fajitas, and Texas beef chili. If you strolled into a restaurant in the interior of Mexico, you shouldn't expect a basket of tortilla chips, salsa, and a combination Mexican food plate, because those are pure Tex-Mex.

In this chapter we are going to look at the essential Tex-Mex dishes that you need to know how to prepare if you want to eat like a proper Texan. You have to start every Tex-Mex meal with bowls of queso and avocado salsa and a basket of hot tortilla chips. I've included a recipe for puffy tortilla chips, but if you don't have the time to make these, just buy a bag of good-quality tortilla chips at the supermarket. There are both good green and roasted red salsa recipes in the Stocks and Sauces chapter, so make plenty for snacking and keep a batch in the refrigerator for emergencies.

Here you'll learn how to make two different types of enchiladas, tacos, chiles rellenos, and a couple of classic Tex-Mex casseroles. For dessert, serve up a creamy Tres Leches Cake (page 232) or Carmelita Bars (page 216) topped with a little vanilla ice cream. What else could a person need?

[Roasting Chiles]

There are more than 150 different varieties of chile peppers. Tex-Mex cooks, however, generally use only a few of these for roasting. The chile most often roasted is the poblano. This dark green chile, the largest of any commonly sold, can be anywhere from mild to hot and has an earthy flavor when roasted. The **Anaheim** chile, also known as the California chile, is also very popular because of its sweet, mild flavor. A cousin to the Anaheim is the much hotter **New Mexico** chile, which is a mainstay in the Mexican food of New Mexico and parts of West Texas. Now stay with me: the **Hatch** chile is a type of New Mexico chile grown in Hatch, New Mexico. Because of the soil and climate of that region, it has a more pronounced flavor than the others.

The skin on all these chiles is a little tough, so it is common to remove it. Most folks char the skin first by putting the chiles directly over the flame of a gas burner. You can also place the chiles under a broiler in the oven or over the fire of a barbecue pit. In restaurants, cooks often fry them to blister their skin. After the skin has been evenly charred, place the chiles in a paper bag or a bowl covered with plastic wrap to steam for about 20 minutes. At this point, if the chiles have a good char, the skin can be scraped off fairly easily. Next, make a cut down the side of the chile and remove the seedpod connected to the stem. Rinse the chiles under cold water, being careful not to rip them. The chiles are now ready to stuff for rellenos, or you can remove the stem before using the chiles in a sauce or puree. When it's Hatch chile season, I'll roast a big batch of the chiles, eat all that I can for a couple of weeks, and freeze the rest to use throughout the year.

Beef Chiles Rellenos in Spicy Tomato Broth

Some chiles rellenos are coated with a batter made of beaten egg whites with the yolks folded in, resulting in something like a fried omelet coating. To me, however, this sort of eggy batter overpowers the chile and its filling. A great chile relleno should feature a light and uncomplicated batter, and the sauce should complement the stuffed chile. So, if you use this recipe as starting point for experimenting with stuffing chiles, I think you will probably end up right back where you started, like I have: with simple beef chiles rellenos in a spicy tomato broth.

MAKES 8 SERVINGS

8 poblano chiles, roasted and peeled

1 pound Beef Chile Relleno Filling (page 154)

1¼ cups all-purpose flour

½ cup cornmeal

1 teaspoon baking powder

½ cup teaspoon salt

1 cup milk

2 eggs

Vegetable oil, for frying

2 cups Spicy Tomato Broth (page 154)

Preheat your oven to 200°F.

Make a small slit in the side of each chile, just under the stem. Fill each chile with the beef filling, being careful not to overstuff and split the chiles.

To make the batter, combine the flour, cornmeal, baking powder, and salt in a mixing bowl. In another large bowl, whisk together the milk and eggs. Fold the dry ingredients into the milk mixture until it forms a smooth batter.

Pour the vegetable oil to a depth of about 2 inches in a large skillet and heat to 350°F to 375°F. Dip each stuffed chile into the batter and gently transfer to the hot oil. Fry the first side until golden brown, about 2 minutes, then turn the rellenos over and fry the second side until golden brown and warmed through. Keep the chiles warm in the oven until you are ready to serve.

To serve the rellenos, ladle about ¼ cup of the tomato broth into the bottom of each shallow bowl and top with a fried chile.

(continued on next page)

(Beef Chiles Rellenos in Spicy Tomato Broth, continued)

BEEF CHILE RELLENO FILLING

MAKES 8 SERVINGS

1½ pounds beef brisket, excess fat removed

4 cups water

4 ancho chiles, stemmed and seeded

1 yellow onion, coarsely chopped

2 plum tomatoes, cored and coarsely chopped

2 cloves garlic

1 tablespoon brown sugar

1 tablespoon coriander seeds, toasted and ground

1 teaspoon dried oregano leaves

2 teaspoons kosher salt

2 teaspoons freshly ground black pepper

Combine all the ingredients in a stockpot and bring to a simmer. Cover and slowly simmer until the brisket is fork-tender and falling apart, about 3 hours. Using tongs or slotted spoon, remove the brisket from the cooking liquid and allow to cool at room temperature. Meanwhile, remove the solids from the cooking liquid using a slotted spoon and transfer the solids to a blender. Add 1 cup of the cooking liquid, puree until it forms a smooth sauce, and set aside.

Cut the brisket across the grain into 2-inch strips. With two forks, shred the brisket into small pieces and place the pieces in a bowl. Stir the reserved puree into the brisket, taste, and adjust the seasoning, if needed.

SPICY TOMATO BROTH

MAKES ABOUT 2 CUPS

1 tablespoon olive oil

1 medium yellow onion, coarsely chopped

4 cloves garlic, coarsely chopped

1 jalapeño, stemmed, seeded, and coarsely chopped

4 cups ripe tomatoes, cored and diced

Salt and freshly ground black pepper

1 teaspoon sugar

2 tablespoons chopped cilantro

1 tablespoon white wine vinegar

2 cups chicken stock

1 tablespoon tomato paste

Heat a saucepan over medium-high heat and add the olive oil. Add the onion, garlic, and jalapeño and sauté until the onion begins to soften, about 2 minutes. Add the tomatoes, season with salt and pepper, add the sugar, and cook until the tomatoes collapse and become soft, about 4 minutes. Add the cilantro, vinegar, chicken stock, and tomato paste and bring to a simmer. Reduce the heat to low and cook until reduced by one-third, for 20 to 30 minutes. Using a food mill with the coarse disk, grind the liquid and solids into a small saucepan. Taste, adjust the seasoning, if needed, and keep warm until ready to serve.

THE BEST WAY TO JUDGE A MEXICAN RESTAURANT is by its chiles rellenos. Traditionally, chiles rellenos are made with poblano peppers that are stuffed with cheese or meat, coated with a batter that's been lightened with egg, and then panfried or deep-fried and served with some type of tomato sauce. In New Mexico, Hatch chiles are often used, and in parts of West Texas they sometimes use dried chiles. I think a good chile relleno is filled with either a good creamy cheese—panela and Oaxaca cheeses are traditional, but Monterey Jack will also work—or a spicy meat filling, such as beef picadillo with raisins and nuts. I have also had some exceptional shrimp rellenos with a brandied walnut cream sauce.

Spanish Rice

Every Mexican joint in the States serves a version of Spanish rice alongside its refried beans and enchiladas or tacos. It wasn't until I went down the path of trying to make Spanish rice at home that I discovered the little subtleties that can make this rice dish great, or doom it to the dog bowl. When visiting San Miguel de Allende, Mexico, I was invited to join friends at their home for a memorable lunch of chicken mole enchiladas served with Spanish rice. After lunch, I went to the kitchen and had the cook teach me how she had made the perfectly cooked rice. This is that simple recipe.

MAKES 6 SERVINGS

3 tablespoons olive oil

2 cups long-grain white rice

1/4 small yellow onion, finely diced

4 cups chicken stock

2 ripe plum tomatoes, cored and coarsely chopped

1 teaspoon kosher salt

1/2 teaspoon finely ground black pepper

2 cups long-grain white rice

1 bay leaf

Heat a sauté pan over medium-high heat and add the olive oil. Add the rice and cook, stirring continually, until it just begins to brown, 2 minutes. Add the onion and cook until the rice is an even light brown and the onion is soft and cooked through, about 2 minutes more. Set aside.

In a large saucepan, combine the chicken stock, tomatoes, salt, and pepper and bring to a simmer. Transfer the mixture to a blender and puree until smooth. Add the mixture back to the saucepan and add the bay leaf and browned rice. Taste the broth and adjust the seasoning, if needed. Bring the rice to a simmer, cover the pot, and cook on low heat for 18 minutes. Fluff the cooked rice with a fork and keep warm until ready to serve.

Creamy Chicken Casserole with Hatch Chiles

A mainstay at our dinner table when I was a kid was my mother's King Ranch Casserole. While the vintage 1970s recipe calls for canned soup and leftover roasted chicken, this version with from-scratch mushroom cream sauce puts this casserole over the top while staying true to the original. If you don't have the time to poach the chicken, use 3 cups of roasted chicken from the supermarket and sauté the onion, celery, and garlic before adding to the sauce. It's a great make-ahead casserole that freezes well; just defrost it overnight before baking. Serve this casserole with plenty of salsa and fried corn tortillas.

MAKES 6 TO 8 SERVINGS

POACHED CHICKEN

1 (3 to 3½-pound) whole chicken

1 yellow onion, diced medium

2 stalks celery, diced medium

2 cloves garlic, minced

1 bay leaf

1 teaspoon dried oregano

2 teaspoons kosher salt

2 teaspoons freshly ground black pepper

2 cups chicken broth

2 cups water

CASSEROLE

2 tablespoons olive oil

2 cups button mushrooms, finely diced

Kosher salt and freshly ground black pepper

3 tablespoons unsalted butter

¼ cup all-purpose flour

1 (10-ounce) can diced tomatoes and chiles with the liquid

1 cup sour cream

½ teaspoon ground cumin

Pinch of freshly grated nutmeg

3 to 4 Hatch chiles or your favorite green chiles, roasted, peeled, and finely diced

¼ bunch cilantro, chopped

18 corn tortillas

2 cups shredded cheddar cheese

1 cup shredded Monterey Jack cheese

Add all the ingredients for the poached chicken to a stockpot. If the liquid doesn't cover the chicken, add a little more water. Bring to a slow boil, reduce the heat to a gentle simmer, and cook the chicken for 4 minutes. Cover the stockpot, cook for 1 minute more, then turn the heat off and let the stockpot sit on the stove, covered, for 1 hour (don't lift the lid or you will lose all your heat). After 1 hour, remove the bay leaf and discard. Remove the chicken and allow to cool at room temperature before removing the bones and skin and cutting the meat into a large dice. Strain the poaching liquid, reserving the solids—onion, celery, and garlic—and 2½ cups of the stock for the casserole. Any extra stock should be saved for use later in soups and sauces.

Preheat your oven to 350°F.

To prepare the casserole, in a large, heavy skillet, heat the olive oil over high heat. Add the mushrooms in a single layer and allow to lightly brown, about 2 minutes, before stirring; continue to cook for 2 minutes more. Season the mushrooms with salt and pepper and add the butter to the skillet. As soon as the butter has melted, add the flour and stir into the mushrooms. Add the 2½ cups chicken stock and vegetables from the poaching liquid and stir to combine. As soon as the liquid comes to a boil, turn the heat down to low and gently simmer the sauce, stirring occasionally, for 10 minutes. Add the tomatoes, sour cream, cumin, nutmeg, roasted chiles, and cilantro and bring the sauce back to a simmer, cooking for 2 minutes more. Turn the heat off and fold the 3 cups diced chicken into the sauce.

In a large sauté pan over high heat, toast each side of the corn tortillas until they just begin to brown, about 30 seconds per side. In a bowl, stir together the cheddar and Monterey Jack cheeses. Lightly grease a 9 by 13-inch casserole dish with the olive oil and line the bottom with 6 of the toasted tortillas, pushing the tortilla edges about $1/2$ inch up the sides of the dish. Spoon one-third of the chicken cream sauce over the tortillas and top with 1 cup of the cheese mixture. Add two more layers of the tortillas, chicken cream sauce, and cheese. Bake, uncovered, until the top of the casserole is golden brown and the middle is hot and bubbly, about 30 minutes. If the casserole has been made ahead and refrigerated, bake it covered with foil for 15 minutes, then uncover and bake for another 30 minutes, until done.

Chicken Sopes with Roasted Corn Crema

Sopes are little fried masa cakes, usually topped with beans, meats, cheeses, and salsas. They are very much like a corn tortilla, only thicker, with a crisp exterior and a soft, creamy center. Often they are made with crimped edges to help hold the toppings in place, but I don't think that's worth the trouble. You will often see street vendors in Mexico selling ears of roasted corn with shakers of chili powder, freshly cut limes, and tubs of crema for you to slather on top. I've combined these ingredients in the Roasted Corn Crema that you dollop on these tasty chicken sopes.

MAKES 10 SOPES

2 cups instant masa harina

1/2 cup all-purpose flour

1/2 teaspoon baking powder

1 teaspoon kosher salt

2 tablespoons vegetable shortening

1 1/2 cups warm water

Vegetable oil for the pan and for frying

1 1/2 pounds cooked shredded chicken

2 cups Roasted Corn Crema (page 160)

Preheat your oven to 200°F.

In a mixing bowl, combine the masa harina, flour, baking powder, and salt. Add the shortening and warm water and stir to combine into loose dough. Knead the dough until it is evenly moist and smooth. Divide the dough into 10 balls of equal size and cover them with plastic wrap or a moist kitchen towel. To shape the sopes, place a ball of dough between two layers of plastic wrap and flatten with the bottom of a pan or a rolling pin to a diameter of about 4 inches and a thickness of 1/4 inch.

Cooking the sopes is a two-step process. Heat a heavy skillet or a *comal* (Mexican griddle) over medium-high heat and lightly coat with vegetable oil. Cook the sopes, turning once, until light golden brown, about 2 minutes on each side. To finish the sopes, pour vegetable oil to a depth of 2 inches in a skillet and heat over medium-high heat to 350°F. Fry each of the sopes until cooked through and crisp, 2 to 3 minutes, turning once. Transfer the sopes to a platter lined with paper towels.

Keep the sopes warm in the oven until ready to serve. To serve, top each of the sopes with some shredded chicken and a good dollop of the crema.

(continued on next page)

ROASTED CORN CREMA

1 ear of corn

1 tablespoon olive oil

Kosher salt and freshly ground black pepper

1 teaspoon chili powder

1 cup Mexican crema or sour cream

Juice of 1 lime

1 tablespoon chopped cilantro

MAKES 2 CUPS

Start a hot fire in your grill and season the grill grates with a little oil, or preheat your broiler.

Brush the ear of corn with the olive oil and then lightly season with salt, pepper, and the chili powder. Cook the corn on the grill or under the broiler, rotating the corn occasionally so that it cooks evenly, until it is lightly browned, about 10 minutes. Cut the roasted kernels from the cob and place in a mixing bowl.

After the corn has cooled to room temperature, add the crema, lime juice, and cilantro to the bowl and stir to combine. Taste and adjust the seasoning, if needed.

[Masa]

Masa is the Spanish word for dough. In Mexico, masa most often refers to a cornmeal dough. This corn masa is the backbone of Tex-Mex cooking, used in tortillas, chips, tamales, sopas, chalupas, gorditas, and many other Mexican dishes. Masa is available in two forms in supermarkets in Mexico and the Southwestern United States: fresh masa and masa de harina. Both begin by drying kernels of corn and then cooking the dried corn in a solution of water combined with lime or ash. The soaked corn is washed and cleaned, then ground into a dough. The fresh masa can then be dried and ground again to produce masa de harina.

In Mexico and the Southwestern United States, masa is most commonly used for making corn tortillas. Tortillas, or "little cake" in Spanish, are the predominant bread of the people of Mexico. Without tortillas, we couldn't make tortilla chips, enchiladas, flautas, chalupas, or tacos, and there would be no Tex-Mex. Flour tortillas are a more modern invention, sometimes eaten in northern Mexico and very popular with the gringos in America for making burritos.

Green Chile Queso

The first thing you order at a Tex-Mex restaurant, besides a cold beer or a margarita, is a bowl of queso with plenty of chips. This Tex-Mex version of queso is one of those gringo inventions that you will never see when traveling in the interior of Mexico. It's always good to get home to Texas and a big bowl of queso, scooped up on corn tortilla chips or slathered over hot tamales. We add roasted green peppers to our queso, but you can spice it up a little more by adding a few chopped pickled jalapeños.

MAKES 10 TO 12 SERVINGS

1 tablespoon unsalted butter

½ cup finely diced yellow onions

½ cup finely diced tomatoes

½ cup finely diced roasted, peeled, and seeded green chiles, such as poblanos or canned New Mexico Hatch chiles

¼ cup milk

1 pound easy-melt cheese, cut into 2-inch cubes

2 cups shredded Monterey Jack cheese

Salt and white pepper

4 green onions, white and green parts, thinly sliced, for garnish

1 tablespoon coarsely chopped cilantro, for garnish

Warm corn tortilla chips, for serving

In a large saucepan over medium-high heat, melt the butter. When it begins to bubble, add the onion and cook until it begins to turn translucent, about 4 minutes. Add the tomatoes and roasted chiles and cook for another 3 to 4 minutes.

Add the milk to the saucepan and then stir in the easy-melt cheese. Turn the temperature to low and cook, stirring until the cheese is melted and creamy, about 5 minutes. Stir in the Monterey Jack and season with salt and white pepper. When the Monterey Jack has melted, about 2 minutes, transfer to a serving bowl and garnish with the green onion and cilantros. Serve with warm corn tortilla chips for dipping.

Puffy Tortilla Chips

Caro's, a Mexican restaurant near Texas Christian University in Fort Worth, has been serving its obligatory bowl of salsa with puffy tortilla chips since long before I went to college in the neighborhood. I've enjoyed puffy tacos in Mexican restaurants in San Antonio, but I've never run across another place that makes the puffy chips. For special occasions, or if I'm not able to get to Caro's when I get the craving for these chips, I'll break out the tortilla press and make up a batch and serve them with some queso, salsa verde, and avocado salsa.

MAKES 6 SERVINGS

1½ cups corn masa, or more as needed

½ cup all-purpose flour

Kosher salt

1 teaspoon baking powder

1 tablespoon vegetable shortening

1⅓ cups warm water, or more as needed

4 cups vegetable oil

In a large mixing bowl, whisk together the corn masa, flour, ¼ teaspoon salt, and baking powder. Stir in the shortening and warm water until the dough comes together. Work the dough by hand until it is smooth. If the dough is too crumbly, add a little more water. If the dough is too wet and sticky, work in more corn masa. Cover the dough with a kitchen towel and allow to rest for at least 15 minutes.

Divide the dough into 16 equal portions and form into smooth balls with the palms of your hands. Place one of the balls between two layers of plastic wrap, or, better yet, between the two halves of a plastic freezer bag that has had the seams cut away. With a rolling pin or tortilla press, roll or press the dough into a circle about ⅛ inch thick and about 6 inches in diameter. Carefully separate the tortilla from the plastic wrap. Lightly grease a heavy skillet or *comal* (Mexican griddle) over high heat and cook the tortilla until it starts developing a crust on the exterior, 20 to 30 seconds on each side (the tortilla won't be cooked all the way through). Continue to roll out and cook the remainder of the tortillas in the same way.

Pour the vegetable oil into a large skillet and heat to 325°F. Cut each tortilla into quarters and fry in the oil, turning once, until puffy and golden brown, 30 to 45 seconds per side. Using a slotted spoon, transfer the chips to a platter lined with paper towels and lightly season with salt before serving.

Serrano Escabeche

Escabeche can refer either to pickled vegetables or to fish that has been preserved in or flavored with a marinade. In almost all Tex-Mex restaurants, you can order a side of pickled vegetables. You will get either jalapeños or serranos (depending on the region and chef) that have been cooked and marinated in vinegar and spices with carrots, cauliflower, and garlic. These peppers and vegetables are great alongside your favorite Mexican food or grilled steak, or chopped up with some tomatoes for a quick salsa.

MAKES 4 CUPS

½ pound fresh serrano chiles

¼ cup olive oil

1 medium yellow onion, diced medium

2 carrots, peeled and thickly sliced

2 cups cauliflower, cut into florets

6 cloves garlic

2 cups cider vinegar

1 cup water

1 tablespoon kosher salt

1 tablespoon sugar

2 bay leaves

1 teaspoon dried oregano

Make a slit in each chile from just below the stem to ¼ inch from the other end. Heat the oil in a large, deep skillet over medium-high heat. Add the serranos, onion, carrots, cauliflower, and garlic and cook, stirring occasionally to keep the vegetables from browning, until the onion just begins to soften, about 3 minutes.

Add the vinegar, water, salt, sugar, bay leaves, and oregano to the skillet and bring to a boil. Turn the heat down and simmer the mixture for 5 minutes. Transfer the both the vegetables and their cooking liquid to a storage container, cover, and refrigerate. Escabeche keeps in the refrigerator for 4 to 6 weeks.

Smoked Beef Barbacoa Tacos

Barbacoa, sometimes referred to as Mexican barbecue, varies from region to region in Mexico, where it can be made from beef, goat, or lamb. In south Texas, barbacoa is traditionally made from a cow's head or just with the cheek meat. Today Tex-Mex cooks use beef cheek as well as beef brisket and chuck roasts. I like to use chuck roast because it has a great flavor and enough fat to keep the meat moist during the long cooking process.

MAKES 10 TO 12 SERVINGS

1 tablespoon kosher salt

1 tablespoon freshly ground black pepper

2 tablespoons chili powder

1 teaspoon ground cumin

1/2 teaspoon dried oregano

1/4 teaspoon ground allspice

1 teaspoon cider vinegar

2 tablespoons olive oil

1 boneless chuck roast, 4 1/2 to 5 pounds

1 large yellow onion, diced medium

4 cloves garlic, coarsely chopped

Juice of 2 oranges

2 cups water

24 corn or flour tortillas, warmed

2 cups Carmen's Green Salsa (page 247)

2 cups Chunky Avocado Salsa (page 167)

1/2 bunch cilantro, coarsely chopped

1/2 medium yellow onion, finely diced

3 limes, cut into wedges

Set up your smoker to cook at a temperature between 275°F and 300°F. If you are using a charcoal barbecue pit, start a small charcoal fire to one side of the pit and soak some smoking wood chips in water.

In a bowl, stir together the salt, pepper, chili powder, cumin, oregano, allspice, cider vinegar, and olive oil. Use the spice mixture to evenly coat the chuck roast. Add the onion, garlic, orange juice, and water to a small baking pan that will hold the roast and fit into your smoker. Place the roast in the middle of the pan and place it in your smoker. If using a barbecue pit, place the roasting pan on the opposite side of the pit from the fire and add a few wet wood chips on the coals. Hot smoke the roast, maintaining the temperature of the smoker or barbecue pit at between 275°F and 300°F, for 2 hours. Turn the roast over and cook for an additional 2 hours. Occasionally check the level of liquid in the pan, adding water to maintain at least 2 inches of liquid. Remove the roast from the smoker and tightly cover the pan with foil.

Preheat your oven to 325°F.

Place the roasting pan in the oven and cook for 2 hours more. Remove the roast from the pan and slice the meat into 3 by 3-inch pieces. With two forks (or your fingers), shred the meat into bite-size pieces. Moisten the meat with a little of the liquid from the roasting pan.

Serve the barbacoa in a bowl, family-style, with the warmed tortillas and bowls of the green salsa, avocado salsa, cilantro, onion, and lime wedges so diners can assemble their own tacos.

TRADITIONALLY BARBACOA is cooked in pits dug into the earth, with the meat wrapped in banana leaves or wet burlap, a method that smokes and steams the meat at the same time. Most commercial kitchens have gotten away from the earthen pit and are cooking their barbacoa in barbecue pits or smokers with a pot of hot water to create the steam. Instead of using this method, we cook the meat in a pan with seasoning and water to partially braise the meat, which adds the necessary moisture while also adding flavor.

Chunky Avocado Salsa

This is my textured version of guacamole: diced avocado with tomatoes, jalapeños, onion, cilantro, and a big splash of lime juice. The creaminess of the avocado, the punch of the jalapeño, and the tartness of the lime make it the perfect accompaniment or topping for any of your favorite Mexican foods. For an easy variation, add some sweet corn and grilled shrimp for a light summer salad.

MAKES 6 TO 8 SERVINGS

3 large ripe avocados

2 plum tomatoes, cored and finely diced

1 jalapeño, stemmed, seeded, and finely diced

1/2 small red onion, finely diced

3 green onions, white and green parts, thinly sliced

1/4 bunch cilantro, chopped

Juice of 2 large limes, plus a little more if storing the salsa

Kosher salt and freshly ground black pepper

Halve the avocados, remove the pits, and, with the tip of a knife, cut the avocado halves into a 1/4-inch crosshatch pattern, cutting down to the skin but not through it. With a large spoon, scoop out the avocado and put it into a mixing bowl.

Add the tomatoes, jalapeño, red and green onions, and cilantro to the avocado and gently stir once or twice to combine. Add the lime juice, olive oil, salt, and pepper, and stir again just until combined. The avocado salsa is best served right away. If storing it, squeeze a little fresh lime juice over the top and cover with plastic wrap, pressing the wrap onto the surface of the salsa to keep it from browning.

Spicy Pork Tamale Gratin

Most folks think of tamales as those heavy things made with corn masa dough and a spicy meat filling that come on every Tex-Mex combination plate. A properly crafted tamale, though, can be a magical thing, with light and fluffy dough and a filling of anything from cheese, beans, and chiles to almonds, raisins, and ricotta. My favorite is, and always has been, a classic pork tamale. I have fancied up and converted our recipe for pork tamales into a gratin that is a lot easier to pull off than the traditional business of filling and steaming corn husks. This is a great dish to take to a potluck dinner or for feeding a big family. Serve with plenty of corn tortilla chips and salsa.

MAKES 8 TO 10 SERVINGS

6½ cups chicken stock

1½ cups cornmeal

¾ cups instant corn masa

1 teaspoon kosher salt

1 teaspoon freshly ground black pepper

6 tablespoons unsalted butter

1½ cups corn kernels

6 green onions, white and green parts, finely chopped

2 eggs

2 cups shredded cheddar cheese

Vegetable oil for the casserole dish

2½ pounds Spicy Pork Filling (page 171)

Preheat your oven to 350°F.

In a large saucepan, whisk together the chicken stock, cornmeal, corn masa, salt, and pepper and place over high heat. Cook, slowly stirring, until the mixture comes to a slow boil, about 5 minutes. Turn the heat down to a simmer and continue cooking until the cornmeal thickens, about 5 minutes. Turn off the heat and stir in the butter, corn kernels, and green onions. Next add the eggs and 1 cup of the cheese, stirring to combine.

Grease a 9 by 13-inch casserole dish and pour one-third of the cornmeal mixture into the casserole, spreading it evenly to cover the bottom of the dish. Evenly spread the pork filling on top, then evenly spoon the remaining cornmeal mixture on top of the pork, smoothing the top with the back of a spoon. Sprinkle the remaining 1 cup cheese on the top of the casserole and place the casserole dish on a baking sheet. Bake in the middle of the oven until bubbly in the middle and golden brown on top, about 30 minutes. If the casserole has been made ahead and refrigerated, bake it covered with foil for 15 minutes, then uncover and bake for another 30 minutes, until done. Allow the tamale gratin to rest for at least 15 minutes before serving.

SPICY PORK FILLING

MAKES ABOUT 5 CUPS

4 guajillo chiles, stemmed and seeded

2 plum tomatoes, cored and coarsely chopped

1 teaspoon dried oregano

1 teaspoon ground cumin

2 teaspoons salt

2 teaspoons freshly ground black pepper

3 cups water

1 tablespoon cider vinegar

2 tablespoons vegetable oil

2¹/₂ pounds pork butt, cut into 3-inch dice

1 medium yellow onion, cut into ¹/₄-inch julienne strips

4 cloves garlic, coarsely chopped

Heat a large sauté pan over medium-high heat and toast the chiles in the pan, about 1 minute on each side, until blistered and aromatic. Place the toasted chiles in a saucepan with the tomatoes, oregano, cumin, salt, pepper, water, and vinegar, bring to a low simmer, and cook for 2 minutes. Cover the pan, turn off the heat, and let the peppers steep for about 30 minutes to soften. Transfer the peppers and all the liquid to a blender and puree until smooth.

Preheat your oven to 350°F.

Heat a heavy Dutch oven over high heat and add the vegetable oil. Add the pork, onion, and garlic and cook until the meat begins to brown and the onion softens, about 4 minutes. Stir in the guajillo puree and bring the mixture to a simmer. Cover the pan and transfer to the oven, cooking until the pork begins to fall apart, 2 to 2¹/₂ hours. Remove the pork from the oven and, using a large fork, shred the pork into the liquid in the bottom of the pan. The pork will continue to absorb the liquid after it is shredded.

Stacked Chili Con Carne Enchiladas with Fried Eggs

In West Texas and parts of New Mexico, you will often be served the stacked enchiladas, with the tortillas arranged flat on a plate and layered with filling and sauce. I learned to make this sauce while working in San Antonio. Here's a classic San Antonio Tex-Mex beef enchilada gravy, meat cooked with onions and chili powder in a chicken stock that is thickened with flour. A stacked enchilada makes the perfect platform for a fried egg. If the French can put a poached egg on a salad, why can't we put fried eggs on our enchiladas? In West Texas, when you want to get fancy with a dish, just slap a fried egg on top of it.

MAKES 4 SERVINGS

¼ cup vegetable oil

1 pound ground beef

1 medium yellow onion, finely diced

4 cloves garlic, minced

¼ cup dark chili powder, preferably ancho chili powder

1 teaspoon ground cumin

1 teaspoon dried oregano

2 teaspoons kosher salt

1 teaspoon freshly ground black pepper

Pinch of sugar

3 tablespoons all-purpose flour

3 cups chicken stock or water

1 tablespoon tomato paste

12 corn tortillas

3 cups shredded cheddar cheese

4 eggs

Salsa verde (see Carmen's Green Salsa, page 247), for serving

Preheat your oven to 375°F.

To make the chili con carne, heat the vegetable oil in a large skillet over high heat. Add the ground beef, onion, and garlic and cook until the beef has cooked through and the onion begins to soften, about 5 minutes. Add the chili powder, cumin, oregano, salt, pepper, and sugar and cook for another minute. Add the flour, stirring to combine with the meat, then stir in the chicken stock and tomato paste. Bring the chili to a simmer and cook slowly, stirring occasionally, for 15 minutes. If the chili becomes too thick, add a splash of water.

To assemble the enchiladas, heat a sauté pan over medium-high heat and add just enough oil to coat the bottom of the pan. With a pair of tongs or a slotted spoon, place a tortilla in the pan and heat, turning once, until it's soft and pliable, about 1 minute. Place the tortilla on an ovenproof plate and cover with a large spoonful of the chili con carne and a large spoonful of cheese. (If you don't have plates that can be heated to 375°F, you can assemble the stacks on a baking sheet, then transfer them to serving plates when they come out of the oven.) Repeat, stacking two more layers of tortillas, chili, and cheese on top of the first. Once you have the hang of it, repeat the process, building three enchilada stacks on three more serving plates. Place the plates with enchiladas in the oven and heat until the cheese is melted and bubbly, about 15 minutes.

While the enchiladas are in the oven, fry four eggs any way you like them. Place a fried egg on top of each stack of enchiladas and serve with a big bowl of salsa verde on the side.

VEGETABLES & SIDES

ALL THE DISHES IN THIS CHAPTER are hearty fare, because that's the type of food that I grew up eating, that I cook at home for friends, and that our guests love to eat at the restaurant. These dishes are bold enough to serve a group of folks out at the ranch, yet they have been gussied up enough that they will work for a city dinner party.

The types of fresh fruits and vegetables that are available to both professional chefs and home cooks probably have doubled since I started out in the food business. When I started cooking, the standard fare was root vegetables, tomatoes, carrots, broccoli, green beans, and—on good days—asparagus. Now I can pick up the phone and have any vegetable grown in the state of California air freighted to me overnight. I can also go to my local specialty grocer and buy produce from around the world.

Almost all large cities have a weekend farmers' market where local farmers and ranchers sell their fresh seasonal vegetables, dairy, and meat. Even Marfa, Texas, has a Saturday farmers' market!

At the restaurant, and at home, I always try to cook fresh, local, and seasonal vegetables. In the spring and summer, this is pretty easy to do: I make sweet peas sautéed with a little butter and tarragon, tender green beans cooked with smoked bacon and spring onions, or, in the late summer, braised okra and tomatoes. In the winter, I braise a lot of greens, including turnip, collard, and mustard greens. Broccoli and cauliflower also start making an appearance on the menu in the winter, simply sautéed with a lemon and brown butter sauce or served as a crusty brown gratin with a cheesy béchamel sauce. I love to drizzle a good olive oil over carrots, turnips, and onions and roast them in a hot oven until lightly caramelized.

When we're out at the ranch we still eat well, even though we can't get a lot of fresh produce. Achiote-Seared Chickpeas (page 179), made with caramelized onions, Green Chile Grits (page 183), Corn and Cheddar Pudding (page 190), and Sugar-and-Tomato Baked Beans (page 181) are among the things you can enjoy even if you are thirty miles from the nearest small town. When fresh local produce is not available, there is nothing wrong with using canned or frozen. Today vegetables are quickly frozen right after harvest at their peak of freshness and flavor. In December, I would much rather use a quality can of chopped tomatoes than a fresh tomato that tastes like watery cardboard.

When prepared properly, potato dishes can be elegantly simple, using only a few ingredients, such as cream, butter, and seasonings. The Loaded Garlic Mashed Potatoes (page 184) are elevated by the addition of garlic and some simple toppings. Whether you're feeding the family or out-of-town guests, Parmesan Potato Gratin (page 189) is the perfect potato to go with a grilled steak, roast beef, or braised pork loin. Take the time to read my tips on the proper method for mashing potatoes.

When I get invited to potluck dinners, there are three dishes available at my restaurant that I am always asked to bring. The Three-Cheese Macaroni with Country Ham (page 191) is usually the first dish to disappear from the buffet, so I've learned to be the first in line. When the gang is grilling steaks, I always bring the Ricotta Spinach Gratin (page 185), featuring chopped spinach in a creamy béchamel sauce with ricotta and Parmesan cheeses. For barbecues, the perfect side is our Sugar-and-Tomato Baked Beans (page 181), a dish of navy beans slowly cooked in a Dutch oven with brown sugar, molasses, onions, and tomatoes.

As I do with all of my cooking, I try to keep my vegetable and side dishes simple and approachable, both for the folks who are cooking them, and, more to the point, for my guests who are eating them. These are the foods that our grandmothers cooked, and recipes that we are glad are still put on the table.

Grilled Asparagus with Broken Tomato Vinaigrette

This is the perfect side dish to serve with some grilled steaks or fish. The asparagus takes only minutes to cook through over a hot fire, and the tomato vinaigrette can be made ahead and then brought out and served at room temperature. Medium to large asparagus work best in this dish, since you can get a nice grilled flavor without overcooking them. If you don't have cherry tomatoes, you can use any good vine-ripened tomato for the vinaigrette. The asparagus can also be served cold, with the spears cut into thirds and tossed with the tomato vinaigrette.

MAKES 8 SERVINGS

2 pounds asparagus, stalk ends trimmed

2 tablespoons olive oil

2 tablespoons balsamic vinegar

Kosher salt and freshly ground black pepper

Broken Tomato Vinaigrette

Start a hot fire in your grill and season the grill grates with a little oil.

In a large bowl, toss the asparagus with the olive oil and balsamic vinegar to lightly coat. Season with salt and black pepper. Grill the asparagus over a medium-hot fire until it reaches al dente texture, about 3 to 4 minutes, or to your desired degree of doneness. The asparagus will continue to cook after it is removed from the grill, so take them off the heat when they are still a little al dente.

Arrange the asparagus on a serving platter or individual plates, spoon the vinaigrette over the top, and serve immediately.

BROKEN TOMATO VINAIGRETTE

MAKES 2 CUPS

¼ cup olive oil

2 shallots, halved and then cut into thin julinenne strips

2 cloves garlic, finely diced

2 cups cherry tomatoes, halved

Kosher salt and freshly ground black pepper

2 teaspoons coarsely chopped fresh oregano

2 teaspoons coarsely chopped flat-leaf parsley

3 tablespoons white wine vinegar

Heat a large skillet over high heat and add the olive oil. Add the shallot and sauté until soft and slightly browned, about 3 minutes. Add the garlic and cook for about 30 seconds before adding the tomatoes to the pan in a single layer. Sear the tomatoes until they begin to collapse, about 2 minutes, before stirring and continuing to cook for another minute. The tomatoes should be soft but still hold together. Remove the skillet from the heat, season the tomatoes with salt and pepper, and stir in the oregano, parsley, and vinegar. Transfer to a bowl until ready to serve. If you like, you can make it up to 1 day ahead, store covered in the refrigerator and bring to room temperature for serving.

Achiote-Seared Chickpeas

The camp cook at the ranch, Lilo, would cook three meals a day for the cowboys working cattle during summer round-ups. He cooked all the meals over an open fire with big cast-iron skillets and Dutch ovens. One of his standard side dishes at dinner was hominy sautéed with garlic and onion and a lot of ground red chiles. He would top it off with a little cheddar cheese to give it just the right balance of heat and creaminess. When we opened the first Lambert's in Austin, I remembered Lilo's dish and decided to fancy it up a bit. I substituted chickpeas for the corn hominy and started them in an achiote oil to give them a little more depth. I tried to stay true to the original version until I got to the arugula, lemon, and goat cheese, but I think Lilo would approve. These chickpeas are great as a snack or as a side dish with a grilled steak or slow-roasted piece of meat.

MAKES 6 SERVINGS

6 tablespoons Achiote Oil (see recipe)

2 cloves garlic, coarsely chopped

3 cups cooked chickpeas

2 tablespoons dark chili powder

Kosher salt and freshly ground black pepper

Oven-Roasted Tomatoes (page 180), coarsely chopped

Caramelized Onion (page 180)

Juice of 1 lemon

3 ounces baby arugula

2 teaspoons coarsely chopped fresh oregano

2 teaspoons coarsely chopped flat-leaf parsley

4 ounces fresh goat cheese

3 pita breads

1 tablespoon olive oil

1 teaspoon toasted cumin seeds, coarsely ground

Heat a large sauté pan over medium-high heat and add the achiote oil. Drop the garlic in the hot oil and swirl the pan so the garlic cooks evenly. As soon as the garlic begins to develop a little color, about 30 seconds, add the chickpeas and turn the heat to high. Allow the chickpeas to sear for about a minute before stirring. Continue to cook until the chickpeas darken slightly and start to sizzle and pop. Stir in the chili powder and lightly season with salt and pepper. Add the tomatoes and onion and continue to cook until they are heated through, about 2 minutes. Squeeze the lemon juice into the chickpeas and remove the pan from the heat. Fold in the arugula, oregano, parsley, and half of the goat cheese. Transfer the chickpeas to a serving platter and crumble the remaining goat cheese over the top. Lightly brush the pitas with olive oil, sprinkle with ground cumin seeds, and toast on a baking sheet in a 375°F oven until light brown, about 5 mintues. Cut into quarters and serve with the prepared chickpeas.

ACHIOTE OIL

1 cup olive oil

2 tablespoons achiote paste

Place the olive oil and achiote paste in a blender and process until smooth. Transfer to a small saucepan and heat to about 200°F; the oil will just begin to ripple. Remove from the heat and allow to steep for at least 30 minutes to 1 hour. Strain the

(continued on next page)

(Achiote-Seared Chickpeas, continued)

oil through a fine-mesh strainer, reserving the oil and discarding any solid bits of achiote. Store, covered, in the refrigerator for up to 6 months.

OVEN-ROASTED TOMATOES

3 plum tomatoes, cored
and halved lengthwise

1 tablespoon olive oil

Kosher salt

Preheat your oven to 225°F.

Place the tomatoes, cut side up, on a baking sheet lined with foil. Lightly drizzle the tomatoes with the olive oil and sprinkle with salt. Roast the tomatoes in the oven until they have lightly browned and most of the liquid has evaporated, 1½ to 2 hours. Store, covered, in the refrigerator, for up to 4 days.

CARAMELIZED ONION

2 tablespoons olive oil

1 medium onion, diced
medium

Kosher salt and freshly
ground black pepper to
taste

Heat a sauté pan over medium-high heat until it's hot, then add the olive oil and onion. Lightly season with salt and pepper. Cook until the onion begins to brown, about 2 minutes, occasionally stirring. Turn the heat to medium and continue cooking, occasionally stirring, until it develops a golden color, about 5 minutes.

ACHIOTE IS A RUST-COLORED SEED harvested from the annatto shrub. The shrub produces pods that contain 40 to 60 seeds each. Achiote seeds impart a mild, earthy pepper flavor and a reddish-yellow color to foods. It's sold in East Indian, Spanish, and Latin American markets as whole seeds, a powder, and a paste.

Sugar-and-Tomato Baked Beans

Thick and syrupy, with a hint of smoke from the bacon and just the right amount of brown sugar and molasses, these beans are ideal for a barbecue or a picnic. A heavy Dutch oven is just right for cooking beans in your oven because it evenly distributes the heat, slowly baking the beans and reducing the liquid to a glaze. If you like really sweet baked beans, double up on the brown sugar. When I'm at the ranch and can't get nice ripe tomatoes, I'll use a can of chopped tomatoes instead, and the beans come out just fine.

MAKES 8 SERVINGS

2 tablespoons olive oil

4 slices smoked bacon, diced small

1 large yellow onion, diced small

3 cloves garlic, minced

4 plum tomatoes, cored and chopped

2 teaspoons kosher salt

1 teaspoon freshly ground black pepper

1 tablespoon paprika

1 teaspoon dried thyme

2 teaspoons mustard powder

1 bay leaf

4 cups water

4 cups chicken stock

1 cup canned tomato sauce

1 pound dried navy beans, picked over and soaked in water overnight

¼ cup firmly packed brown sugar

1 tablespoon molasses

Preheat your oven to 325°F.

Heat a Dutch oven over medium-high heat and add the olive oil and bacon. Cook until the bacon fat has rendered and the bacon is crispy, about 5 minutes. Add the onion and cook until it softens and begins to brown, 3 to 4 minutes. Stir in the garlic and cook for 1 minute. Add the tomatoes, salt, pepper, paprika, thyme, mustard powder, and bay leaf and cook until the tomatoes become soft and collapse, about 4 minutes. Add the water, chicken stock, tomato sauce, beans, brown sugar, and molasses and bring the beans to a boil. Cover the Dutch oven and place in the middle of your oven. Bake the beans for 2 hours, stirring once after the first hour of cooking.

Uncover the pot and continue to bake the beans, stirring occasionally, until the liquid has reduced to a syrupy consistency and the beans are tender, about 30 minutes more. If the beans become too dry during the last hour of cooking, add a little water to the pot. Taste, adjust the seasoning, if needed, and serve the beans hot.

Green Chile Grits

Because I grew up eating grits for breakfast, lunch, and dinner, I assumed that everyone knew what grits were and that they loved a big bowl of them, topped with a little dab of butter, like I do. When I lived in New York and California, though, I discovered that there are people who turn their noses up at the thought of eating grits. Their problem is that they have never eaten my version of grits. You can't go wrong with the flavors of sweet corn, butter, creamy Monterey Jack cheese, and roasted green chiles all swimming together in a big bowl of grits.

MAKES 8 SERVINGS

4 cups milk

1 teaspoon salt

1/2 teaspoon freshly ground black pepper

1 cup grits

4 tablespoons unsalted butter

1/2 cup Green Chile Puree

1 cup shredded Monterey Jack cheese

2 green onions, white and green parts, finely chopped

In a heavy pot, combine the milk, salt, and pepper and bring to a boil. As soon as the milk comes to a boil, gradually whisk in the grits. Turn the heat down to a simmer and slowly cook the grits, stirring occasionally to keep them from sticking, until thick and creamy, 15 to 20 minutes.

Remove the grits from the heat and stir in the butter and chile puree. Fold in the cheese and green onions and serve immediately.

GREEN CHILE PUREE

MAKES 1 CUP

1 large poblano chile, roasted, peeled, and seeded

1/4 cup spinach leaves, stemmed

1/4 cup coarsely chopped flat-leaf parsley

1/4 cup boiling water

Pinch of kosher salt

Combine all the ingredients in a blender and puree until smooth. The puree can be stored, covered, in the refrigerator for up to a week.

Joann's Stewed Okra and Tomatoes

For years we had okra growing behind our house, since the vegetable grows like a weed in the West Texas heat, producing from midsummer all the way into the fall. My mother would pick the small pods every three or four days and then cook up a batch of stewed okra with tomatoes at least once a week. Some folks think that stewed okra is slimy, but they're probably the same folks who think a trout tastes fishy and a piece of venison tastes gamey. It's part of the deal when you eat okra.

MAKES 8 SERVINGS

1¹/₂ pounds small fresh okra

1 tablespoon olive oil

2 tablespoon unsalted butter

1 large yellow onion, thinly sliced

4 cloves garlic, finely chopped

5 plum tomatoes, cored and coarsely diced

1 teaspoon kosher salt

¹/₂ teaspoon freshly ground black pepper

2 teaspoons sugar

¹/₂ teaspoon dried oregano

¹/₂ teaspoon dried basil

¹/₂ cup water

1 tablespoon red wine vinegar

Rinse the okra, trim the tops of the stems, and make a slit from halfway down the okra to the tip; the slit allows the okra to cook through more quickly. Set aside.

Heat a large skillet over medium-high heat and add the olive oil and butter. When the butter has melted, add the onion and sauté until soft, about 4 minutes. Add the garlic and cook for another minute.

Turn the heat to high, add the okra, and stir to combine with the onion and garlic. Cook for 2 minutes and then add the tomatoes. Cook until the tomatoes begin to collapse, about 2 minutes. Add the salt, black pepper, sugar, oregano, and basil. Stir in the water and vinegar and bring to a simmer. Adjust the heat to maintain a vigorous simmer and continue cooking until the okra is tender and most of the liquid has evaporated, about 15 minutes. Transfer to a bowl and serve hot.

Parmesan Potato Gratin

When dining at a big-city steakhouse, I want a char-grilled steak cooked medium-rare and a side of potato gratin, with a cheese-crusted top and a creamy potato center. I love the Parmesan cheese and thyme in these potatoes, but I'll sometimes change it up with Gruyère and a little roasted garlic. The trick to a good potato gratin is to put the potatoes into the cream as you cut them. The cream will keep the cut potatoes from oxidizing—or turning brown—without washing off the potato's starch. The starch helps to thicken the cream and hold the potatoes together when cooked. You can make this gratin ahead of time and reheat it, covered with foil, in a low oven.

MAKES 8 TO 10 SERVINGS

2 tablespoons unsalted butter

3 cups heavy cream

1¹/₂ cups freshly grated Parmesan cheese

2 teaspoons kosher salt

¹/₂ teaspoon white pepper

2 teaspoons coarsely chopped fresh thyme

Pinch of freshly grated nutmeg

3 pounds russet potatoes, peeled

Preheat your oven to 375°F. Lightly grease a 9 by 13-inch casserole dish or a 3-quart Dutch oven with 1 tablespoon of the butter.

In a large mixing bowl, combine the cream, ³/₄ cup of the Parmesan, the salt, white pepper, thyme, and nutmeg. Evenly slice the potatoes ¹/₈-inch thick and place in the bowl with the seasoned cream, stirring to coat the potatoes.

Arrange the potato slices in the casserole dish, overlapping them like shingles on a roof. Pour the cream mixture remaining in the bowl evenly over the potatoes; the cream should come almost to the top layer of potatoes. Press down on the potatoes to evenly compact them into the cream.

Sprinkle the remaining ³/₄ cup Parmesan over the potatoes and then dot the top of the cheese with small pieces of the remaining 1 tablespoon butter. Bake the gratin, uncovered, in the middle of the oven until the potatoes are tender and the top is golden brown, about 1 hour and 15 minutes. Let the gratin rest for at least 15 minutes before serving. If you want to reheat, cover the gratin with foil and place in 275°F oven for at least 40 to 45 minutes.

Corn and Cheddar Pudding

This is my standby recipe when I have to throw together a dish at the last minute. The great thing about this creamy corn pudding is that most of the ingredients are always in the pantry. When fresh corn is in season, I will quickly sauté 4 cups of kernels with a little butter. I use 2 cups of the whole kernels and puree the other half of the corn with a little milk to substitute for both types of canned corn in the recipe. This pudding is also great with some diced roasted green chiles tossed in. Whether you're grilling steaks in the backyard or slow smoking a big sloppy pork butt, your family and friends will love this pudding.

MAKES 10 TO 12 SERVINGS

2 (8-ounce) boxes cornbread mix

¹/₂ cup cornmeal

1 tablespoon sugar

1 teaspoon kosher salt

2 teaspoons freshly ground black pepper

5 eggs

4 cups sour cream

¹/₂ cup unsalted butter, melted

1 (5-ounce) can creamed corn

1 (5-ounce) can corn kernels, drained

1 small yellow onion, finely diced

1 bunch green onions, white and green parts, finely chopped

1 pickled jalapeño, finely diced

2 cups shredded sharp cheddar cheese

Preheat your oven to 350°F and lightly grease a 9 by 13-inch casserole dish.

In a large bowl, stir together the cornbread mix, cornmeal, sugar, salt, and pepper. In another bowl, whisk together the eggs, sour cream, and melted butter. Fold the wet ingredients into the cornbread mix until just combined. Add the creamed corn, corn kernels, yellow onion, green onion, and jalapeño and stir to incorporate. Stir in the cheese and transfer the mixture into the casserole dish.

Place the casserole dish in a roasting pan and fill the pan with hot water until it comes halfway up the side of the casserole dish. Bake in the middle the oven until lightly golden brown and the middle of the casserole is firm and cooked through, about 45 minutes. Serve hot.

Three-Cheese Macaroni with Country Ham

At Lambert's, we always use large elbow macaroni, but penne also works great. If any of your gang doesn't like goat cheese—I have a friend who refuses to eat it—you can substitute a white, easy-melt cheese, such as a Swiss or jack.

MAKES 8 TO 10 SERVINGS

1 pound large elbow macaroni

4 tablespoons unsalted butter

3 ounces country ham, prosciutto, or smoked ham, finely diced

1/4 cup all-purpose flour

3 cups whole milk

1/2 teaspoon kosher salt

1/2 teaspoon freshly ground black pepper

Pinch of cayenne pepper

1 cup fresh goat cheese

3 cups shredded sharp cheddar cheese

1 1/4 cups freshly grated Parmesan cheese

1 cup bread crumbs, preferably Japanese panko

Preheat your oven to 350°F. Lightly grease a 9 by 13-inch casserole dish.

Bring a large pot of salted water to a boil. Add the macaroni and cook until al dente, about 8 minutes or according to the package directions. Drain the pasta, rinse with cold water, and set aside in a large mixing bowl.

Heat a large, heavy saucepan over medium-high heat and add the butter. As soon as the butter is melted, add the ham and cook until it starts to turn crispy, about 3 minutes. Stir in the flour and cook for 2 minutes more. Whisk in the milk and bring the sauce to a simmer. Cook at a low simmer until the sauce is smooth and thick, about 4 minutes. Add the salt, black pepper, and cayenne. Add the goat cheese, 1 cup of the cheddar, and 3/4 cup of the Parmesan and stir until the cheeses have melted and the sauce is creamy. Remove the sauce from the heat.

Pour the cheese sauce over the cooked macaroni and stir to evenly coat. Add the remaining 2 cups cheddar and stir to combine. Transfer the macaroni to the prepared casserole dish, spreading it out in an even layer.

In a small bowl, stir together the remaining 1/2 cup Parmesan and the bread crumbs and sprinkle evenly over the macaroni. Bake until the center is bubbly and the top is golden brown, about 45 minutes. If the dish has been made ahead and refrigerated, bake it covered with foil for 20 minutes, then uncover it and bake for another 40 to 45 minutes, until done.

I WAS TALKED INTO PARTICIPATING IN A MAC AND CHEESE COOK-OFF, with the proceeds benefiting a children's after-school program. My competitors made everything from small elbow macaroni covered with fake cheese from a jar to penne coated with white wine, Italian herbs, and brie. I never realized there were so many ways to make mac and cheese. I came in second place; it turns out the kids were judging, and they had a fondness for processed cheese. I don't care what the little brats say (I'm a little bitter): this is still my favorite way to make this dish.

Braised Greens with Smoked Ham Hock

The only place you can get a good bowl of greens these days is at a small-town café or when someone's grandmother is cooking for you. There is nothing difficult about cooking greens; just build the flavors with some sautéed onion and garlic, add a ham hock for some pork and smoke goodness, and then cook the greens down until they are as tender as a mother's love. If you can't find a ham hock, sauté a little bacon with the onions and you'll be just fine.

MAKES 8 SERVINGS

2 tablespoons olive oil

1 large yellow onion, diced medium

4 cloves garlic, finely chopped

2 cups chicken stock

2 cups water

2 tablespoons cider vinegar

3 pounds mustard, turnip, or collard greens or kale, stemmed and cut into 2-inch strips

1 tablespoon kosher salt

1 teaspoon freshly ground black pepper

1 tablespoon sugar

1 smoked ham hock

Heat a large, heavy pot over medium-high heat and add the olive oil. Add the onion and cook until soft, about 4 minutes. Stir in the garlic and continue to cook for another minute. Pour the chicken stock, water, and vinegar into the pot and bring to a boil. Add the greens in batches; as the greens wilt into the hot liquid, continue putting them in the pot until they have all been added. Add the salt, pepper, sugar, and ham hock. When the liquid has returned to a boil, turn the heat down to a simmer. Partially cover the pot and slowly simmer, stirring occasionally, until the greens are tender, about 1 hour. Transfer to a bowl and serve.

COUNTRY HAM IS A CURED HAM from the southern United States. They are salt-cured for one to three months and then usually smoked for added flavor, though they do not have to be smoked to be called a country ham. After curing, the hams are aged anywhere from several months to two to three years. This curing and aging process produces a ham that is very salty and somewhat dense. The hams are soaked in water and the salt and the mold scrubbed off before they are cooked whole or sliced and panfried. A country ham is similar to a leg of Italian prosciutto, but prosciutto is not smoked and typically a little moister. Country hams are usually sold as unrefrigerated bone-in hams wrapped in cotton or burlap bags.

KITCHEN
Local Goods and Products

Cooper Orchards BOGGY CREEK FARMS
Pure Luck COUNTRY SIDE FARMS San Miguel SEAFOOD
Cheeses BLUEBONNET HYDROPONICS YOAKUM Heartbrand BEEF
Veldhuizen Farms Kevin Roberts FARM EGGS HOUSTON DAIRY MAIDS
MOONLIGHT Bakery

ser Tees 20
Caps 20
of Rubs 15

Upcoming...
7:30 Residencies
NO COVER
WED. the MOONHANGE
THURS. Lee Mork GAP CL
FRI. JITTERBUG VIPERS
SAT. CONTINENTAL GRAF
SUN. black, red, black

BREADS

AS A GUY WHO WORKS AROUND FOOD for a living, I have more respect for baking (and for the folks who have made a profession of baking) than for anything else that has to do with a kitchen. Sure, there are chefs who squirt foams onto their food, paint sauces on plates, or serve silly deconstructed food, but all of this is child's play compared to the work of a baker who can make a perfect loaf of bread out of nothing more than flour, yeast, and water. The only thing most fancy-pants chefs know about bread is that a corned beef sandwich is best served on rye.

In a professional kitchen, there are usually two distinct worlds—that of chefs and cooks, who prepare meats, sauces, and vegetables, and that of the bakers, who make the desserts and breads—and these two worlds seldom intersect. The reason most chefs and cooks can't or won't bake is that they are trained to cook from their gut, using their instinct for taste and texture. Bakers, on the other hand, are more cerebral and spiritual. They have to know and follow time-tested formulas and ratios for what they are baking. They also have to develop an instinct for different types of batter and dough, learning how they should look and feel. There is nothing more graceful than a seasoned bread baker in full swing forming loaves of bread. Cooking may be an art, but baking is both an art *and* a science.

A lot of cooks are a little intimidated by the baking process, probably because they haven't really been exposed to it. For older generations, baking was a part of the daily kitchen routine. Today, however, most folks buy their biscuits in a cardboard tube and their rolls from the frozen foods section of the grocery store. We should all slow down, break out the flour, and turn on our ovens. Becoming a solid baker is as easy as understanding a recipe's ingredients and their proper mixing method (the science) and, more importantly, practicing enough to develop a feel for the dough (the art).

In this chapter, we are going to look at two basic types of bread: quick breads and yeast breads. Quick breads, such as muffins and biscuits, don't require kneading or time to proof. The primary leavenings used in quick breads are baking soda and baking powder. Baking soda is used when the dough contains an acidic ingredient like buttermilk, sour cream, yogurt, or lemon. When the soda comes in contact with the acid, carbon dioxide is produced, which causes the dough to rise. Baking powder is made up of baking soda and a powdered acid, like cream of tarter. Almost all baking powders are double-acting, which means that carbon dioxide is released both when the powder is mixed with liquid and again when it is exposed to heat. Baking powder is perishable and best kept in a dry, dark place in your kitchen. To test it to see if it still has its punch, combine a teaspoon of the baking powder with $1/2$ cup warm water. If the bowl bubbles like a hot tub, you're good to go.

Eggs and butter act as additional leavening ingredients in quick breads. Eggs cause baked goods to rise when the water in the whites turns into steam and expands. As the steam causes the dough to rise, the proteins in the egg whites coagulate, forming structure for the bread. Butter leavens breads in much the same way, as the water in the butter turns to steam in the heat of the oven. When making biscuits, for example, cold butter is cut or worked into the flour until it forms pea-size pieces. When the dough is rolled out, then, the cold butter flakes are layered in the flour. When the heat hits the biscuits, the water in the butter is turned to steam and causes the dough to rise.

Yeast breads can be anything from a crusty French baguette to a fluffy dinner roll. Yeast not only acts as the leavening agent in these breads, but it also gives them a unique flavor. Yeast is a living organism that we cause to reproduce by giving it food, a warm environment, and time. The yeast consumes the sugars in a dough and converts them into carbon dioxide and alcohol. The wheat flour used in most breads is made up of starchy proteins, called gluten, that produce both the stretchy framework of the bread as well as food for the yeast to consume. The yeast also produces carbon dioxide, which stretches the dough until it forms air pockets, while the alcohol flavors the bread. Most bread recipes contain sugar, which not only sweetens the finished bread but gives the yeast extra food to speed up the time it takes the bread to proof and rise.

[Yeast]

There are three primary types of yeast available to home bakers in the grocery store. **Active dry yeast** is made by drying live yeast cultures into dormant granules. To use the yeast, the granules are first revived by adding them to warm water (105°F to 110°F) with a pinch of sugar. If unopened, active dry yeast can be kept for up to a year at room temperature, or longer if frozen. Once opened, it should be refrigerated and used within about three months. **Instant yeast** is sold under a few different names, including rapid-rise, quick-rise, and bread machine yeast. Instant yeast works about 50 percent faster than active dry yeast, doesn't need to be reactivated in warm water, and can be used interchangeably, in the same amount, as active dry yeast. Instant yeast can be stored like active dry yeast and has about the same shelf life. **Fresh yeast** is made by mixing live yeast cells with cornstarch and compressing the yeast into cakes. Fresh yeast must be stored in the refrigerator and has a shelf life of about 2 weeks. It is the most active (gas producing) of all the yeasts, which means it is best able to make bread rise and give it a great flavor. When using fresh yeast, activate it in warm water (90°F) before adding it to the rest of your ingredients. A 2-ounce cake of fresh yeast is equal to three ¹/₄-ounce packets of active dry yeast.

Regardless of the type of yeast you are using, temperature is the key factor in its growth. The perfect temperature for promoting an active yeast is 95°F. Some bakers, though, proof their breads at a lower temperature, around 80°F, because it slows the proofing process, which in turn produces higher levels of alcohol and a more flavorful bread. The lower the temperature, the less active the yeast. That is why bakers will refer to the refrigerator as a "retarder": refrigeration retards the growth of yeast. On the other end, high temperatures will kill your yeast. By adding a liquid that is hotter than 120°F or proofing your bread in an extremely hot area of your kitchen, you run the risk of killing off the yeast in your dough.

Brunch Buttermilk Biscuits

We do a big Sunday brunch at the restaurant, when we always serve up baskets of warm buttermilk biscuits. Nothing is as welcoming and comforting as light and fluffy homemade biscuits, ready for some butter and jam or a slathering of peppery gravy. The trick to tender biscuits is to mix them with a light hand, without overworking the dough. If you want to jazz up this recipe a little, add some cheddar cheese and chopped green onions to the dough.

MAKES 12 BISCUITS

3 cups all-purpose flour

2 teaspoons salt

1 tablespoon baking powder

2 teaspoons baking soda

1 tablespoon sugar

6 tablespoons cold unsalted butter, cut into small pieces

1½ cups buttermilk

Preheat your oven to 425°F and lightly grease a baking sheet.

In a large bowl, whisk together the flour, salt, baking powder, baking soda, and sugar. Add the cold butter and, using a pastry cutter or your fingers, work the butter into the flour until the mixture resembles coarse meal. With a rubber spatula, fold in the buttermilk until the dough just comes together.

Transfer the dough to a lightly floured work surface. Lightly dust the top of the dough with flour and, using a rolling pin, roll out to about 3/4 inch thick. Cut out biscuits with a 2½-inch biscuit cutter and place on the baking sheet about 1/4 inch apart. Gather up any scraps of dough and gently fold together. Roll out again and cut out a few more biscuits.

Bake the biscuits until they are golden brown, about 15 minutes. Serve immediately.

Buttery Parker County Dinner Rolls

This is the simple yeast roll that my grandmother served at dinner came from a Parker County cookbook. These sweet, buttery rolls are perfect for pushing meat onto your fork or sopping up gravy—never mind proper manners. When I make these rolls at home, I prepare a double batch of the dough. Half of them I bake and serve at once, and the other half I bake just until they begin to get a little color—about 8 minutes—before I cool and freeze them. Then, when I need homemade rolls on short notice, I just let them thaw on the counter for about 30 minutes and then finish baking until they are golden brown.

MAKES 16 DINNER ROLLS

1³/₄ cups whole milk

¹/₂ cup unsalted butter, plus 2 tablespoons for brushing

¹/₄ cup sugar

5 cups all-purpose flour, plus a little more for kneading

2 teaspoons kosher salt

1 tablespoon active dry yeast

In a small saucepan or microwave-safe bowl, combine the milk, butter, and sugar. Using your stove or a microwave oven, heat the mixture just until warm enough to melt the butter, about 95°F. Stir together the flour, salt, and yeast in the bowl of your stand mixer with the dough hook attachment. Turn the mixer on low and add the milk mixture. Once the dough comes together, about 30 seconds, turn the mixer to medium and work the dough for about 5 minutes. If the dough is too wet and will not come together after 1 or 2 minutes of mixing, gradually add a little more flour until a proper dough is formed.

Transfer the dough to a work surface lightly dusted with flour and form it into a compact ball. Lightly coat a large mixing bowl with vegetable oil, place the dough in the bowl, and cover with plastic wrap. Allow the dough to proof in a warm place in your kitchen until it has doubled in volume, about 1 hour.

Transfer the proofed dough from the bowl to a lightly floured work surface. Punch down the dough and divide into 16 pieces of equal size, each about 2¹/₂ ounces. With a cupped hand, roll each of the dough pieces into a compact ball.

Lightly grease a 9 by 9-inch baking pan with butter and place the rolls in the pan in 4 rows of 4. Cover the rolls with a dish towel and let them rise in a warm place again for about 45 minutes.

Preheat your oven to 350°F. Bake the rolls on the middle rack until golden brown, 12 to 15 minutes. Remove the rolls from the oven, brush with a little melted butter, and serve immediately.

Citrus Scones

Scones are really nothing more than fancy biscuits, and you don't have to be a lady in a big hat or a tea-sipper to enjoy them. As soon as we opened Jo's in Austin, these scones became a mainstay on the menu. For a savory version, we omit the citrus zest and add a little chopped crispy bacon, roasted green peppers, and cheddar cheese. This dough freezes well; just let the frozen scones defrost in the refrigerator overnight and bake according to the recipe.

MAKES 12 SCONES

4 cups all-purpose flour

3/4 cup sugar, plus more for sprinkling

1 teaspoon plus 1 pinch of salt

1 teaspoon baking powder

1/4 cup orange or lemon zest, or a combination

1 cup cold unsalted butter, cut into small pieces

1 3/4 cups heavy cream

1 egg

2 tablespoons water

Preheat your oven to 375°F.

In a bowl, whisk together the flour, sugar, 1 teaspoon of salt, and the baking powder. Add the citrus zest and stir to combine. Add the cold butter and, using a pastry cutter or your fingers, work the butter into the flour until it forms into pea-sized pieces. With a rubber spatula, gently fold in the cream just until a loose dough comes together.

Transfer the dough to a lightly floured work surface and gently knead the dough just until it comes together in a smooth ball. Lightly dust with flour and, using a rolling pin, roll out into a rectangle about 10 by 14 inches. With the short end of the dough facing you, fold the dough in half, from top to bottom, and roll out again into a 10 by 14-inch rectangle. Repeat this folding and rolling process two more times.

Roll out the dough to a 1-inch thickness and, using a 2 1/2-inch biscuit cutter, cut the dough into rounds. Gather up any scraps of dough and gently fold together. Roll out again and cut out a few more scones. Place the scones on a baking sheet.

To make the egg wash, in a small bowl, whisk together the egg, water, and a pinch of salt. Using a pastry brush, brush each of the scones with the egg wash, and then lightly sprinkle with sugar. Bake until golden brown, about 18 minutes. Let the scones cool on a wire rack for 15 minutes before serving.

Green Onion Skillet Corn Cakes

I like to serve these savory little corn cakes with seafood gumbo or a bowl of chili, or as an appetizer smeared with sour cream and smoked salmon. For a little heat, add a chopped pickled jalapeño pepper to the batter.

MAKES 24 SMALL CAKES

2 cups finely ground yellow cornmeal

1¼ cups all-purpose flour

¼ cup sugar

1 tablespoon baking powder

1 teaspoon baking soda

1 teaspoon salt

6 eggs

2 cups buttermilk

1 (4-ounce) can creamed corn

¼ cup finely chopped green onion, white and green parts

6 tablespoons unsalted butter, melted, plus 1 to 2 tablespoons for the skillet

Preheat your oven to 200°F.

In a bowl, stir together the cornmeal, flour, sugar, baking powder, and baking soda. In another bowl, whisk the eggs until blended. Add the buttermilk and creamed corn to the eggs and whisk together. Add the egg mixture to the dry ingredients and stir to combine. Finally, add the green onions and 6 tablespoons of the melted butter and stir until the batter is smooth.

Heat a large skillet over medium-high heat and add the remaining melted butter to coat the bottom of the pan. Using a large spoon, a 2-ounce ladle, or a ¼-cup measuring cup, pour the batter into the skillet, being careful not to crowd the cakes (you'll have to cook them in batches). Cook until bubbles form and burst on the top of the cakes and the bottoms are golden brown, about 2 minutes. Flip the cakes and brown the other side, about 2 minutes more. Keep the cakes warm in the oven while you finish the other batches. Serve hot.

Jalapeño Corn Muffins

The breads we serve our customers at Lambert's make up a huge part of the overall dining experience, and the star of our bread basket has always been our jalapeño corn muffins. I think this muffin has a great balance of cornmeal and fresh corn, with a savory onion flavor and a jalapeño punch. At Jo's, we serve full-size muffins, as described in this recipe. At Lambert's, we serve a miniature version for easier munching with your barbecue or steak. If you are afraid of the jalapeño (please don't be), you can substitute a milder roasted New Mexico green chile.

MAKES 12 MUFFINS

1 cup cornmeal

1/2 cup sugar

1 cup all-purpose flour

1 tablespoon baking powder

3/4 teaspoon salt

1/4 cup canola oil

1 1/4 cups buttermilk

1 egg

2 tablespoons unsalted butter, melted

1 cup fresh corn kernels, cut from the cob

1 cup shredded cheddar cheese

1/2 cup finely chopped green onions, white and green parts

1/4 cup finely diced yellow onion

1/4 cup seeded and finely diced pickled jalapeños

Preheat your oven to 375°F and grease your muffin tins with nonstick vegetable oil spray.

In a large bowl, stir together the cornmeal, sugar, flour, baking powder, and salt. In a small bowl, combine the oil, buttermilk, and egg and whisk until well blended. Pour the wet mixture into the dry mixture, add the melted butter, and stir to combine. Stir in the corn, cheese, green and yellow onions, and jalapeños.

Evenly distribute the batter among the greased muffin tins and bake until the muffins are golden brown on top, about 18 minutes.

Onion Flatbread

Traditionally, flatbreads are made in Dutch ovens with a sourdough starter that the camp cook has used for years. It's the sourdough that leavens the bread and gives it a unique flavor. Most home cooks don't have a sourdough starter in the cupboard to use when they want to throw together a loaf of bread, so here's a flatbread recipe that begins with fermenting a dough starter, which will give you a loaf of bread with some of the flavor of sourdough. The addition of onion in the fermentation gives the bread a sweet, tangy flavor. Try a variation of this flatbread by adding herbs, Parmesan cheese, or sun-dried tomatoes.

MAKES 1 LOAF

STARTER

1½ cups bread flour

¾ cup finely minced yellow onion

2 teaspoons sugar

1 tablespoon active dry yeast

1 cup water

FLATBREAD

4 cups bread flour

1 tablespoon kosher salt

1 tablespoon sugar

1 teaspoon active dry yeast

3 tablespoons garlic, minced

¼ cup finely chopped green onions, white and green parts

3 tablespoons olive oil, plus more for brushing

1 cup water

To make the starter, combine the flour, onion, sugar, and yeast in a small mixing bowl. Stir in the water, mixing until a wet dough is formed. Cover the bowl with plastic wrap and let it sit on your counter, at room temperature, for 8 hours or overnight.

When your starter has had time to develop and you are ready to make the flatbread, whisk together the flour, salt, and sugar in the bowl of your stand mixer. Add the yeast, garlic, and green onions, again stirring to combine. Add the starter, olive oil, and water. With the dough hook, mix on medium speed for 5 minutes. If the dough is too dry, add a few tablespoons of water until a soft dough comes together.

Transfer the dough to a lightly floured work surface and knead by hand for 2 minutes. When the dough becomes smooth and elastic, form it into a compact ball. Lightly coat a large mixing bowl with olive oil, place the dough in the bowl, and cover with plastic wrap. Allow the dough to proof in a warm place in your kitchen until it has doubled in size, about 1 hour.

Lightly grease a large baking sheet with olive oil. Transfer the proofed dough to the baking sheet, keeping the dough in its nice, uniform, ballooned shape. Push the dough down with the palms of your hands until it forms an oval about 1 inch thick. Brush the top of the dough with olive oil and allow the dough to proof for a second until it has doubled in size again, about 45 minutes.

Preheat the oven to 350°F. Place the bread in the middle of the oven and bake until golden brown, about 20 minutes.

(continued on next page)

(Onion Flatbread, continued)

Remove from the oven and allow to cool for at least 15 minutes before serving.

BEFORE COMMERCIAL YEASTS WERE AVAILABLE, sourdough starters were used by camp cooks to leaven the breads they baked. A sourdough starter is made by mixing flour and water to form a wet dough and allowing naturally occurring bacteria and yeast to ferment the dough. The starter is stable at room temperature and can be kept alive by feeding it additional flour and water during the week. The yeasts in the starter leavens the bread, and the starter's long fermentation gives the bread a unique tangy flavor. A starter that is properly cared for can last for years: some bakeries in San Francisco claim to be using sourdough starters that are 150 years old.

Many artisan bakers use a dough starter, also known as a prefermentation—not an actual sourdough—to add some sourdough flavor to bread. Starters, like the Italian *biga* and French *poolish,* are made by mixing some of the water and flour with yeast and allowing it to ferment for anywhere from half a day to a couple of days.

Governor's Mansion Potato Rolls

We first started making these rolls when we catered a lot of events at the governor's mansion in Texas. The potatoes in these rolls give them a distinctive flavor and an unbelievably light texture. They are great as a dinner roll, but my favorite is to use them for little cocktail sandwiches with roast beef, turkey, or a honey ham.

MAKES 20 ROLLS

5 cups all-purpose flour

3 tablespoons sugar

1 tablespoon active dry yeast

2 teaspoons salt

1 cup mashed potatoes

1 cup whole milk

½ cup unsalted butter, plus 4 tablespoons, melted, for brushing

2 eggs

Stir together 2 cups of the flour, the sugar, and yeast in the bowl of your stand mixer, using a spoon. In another bowl, stir together the remaining 3 cups of flour with the salt.

In a saucepan or microwave-safe bowl, combine the mashed potatoes, milk, and butter. Using your stove or microwave oven, heat the mixture just until warm and the butter is melted, about 100°F. Add the eggs to the potato mixture, and stir to combine. Then add to the flour mixture in your stand mixer. Using the dough hook, mix on low until the dough starts to come together, about 1 minute. With the mixer still running, add the remaining 3 cups of flour, 1 cup at a time. When the dough comes together, turn the mixer to medium and mix until the dough is smooth and elastic, about 5 minutes. If the dough is too moist and does not form a ball during the first two minutes of mixing, gradually add more flour, a couple of tablespoons at a time. You do, however, want a fairly moist dough.

Transfer the dough to a work surface lightly dusted with flour and form into a compact ball. Lightly coat a mixing bowl with vegetable oil, place the dough in the bowl, and cover with plastic wrap. Allow the dough to proof in a warm place in the kitchen until it has doubled in size, about 1 hour.

Line a baking sheet with parchment paper.

Turn the dough out onto a lightly floured work surface. Cut the dough into two pieces, rolling each piece back and forth into a cylinder about 3 inches in diameter. Cut each cylinder into 10 pieces of equal size. Form the rolls by rolling each piece under your cupped hand in a small circle while applying a little pressure. Place the rolls about 2 inches apart on the baking sheet, cover loosely with plastic wrap, and let rise in a warm place again for about 45 minutes.

Preheat your oven to 350°F. Bake the rolls on the middle rack until golden brown, 14 to 18 minutes. Remove the rolls from the oven, brush with the melted butter, and serve immediately.

DESSERTS

WHEN ASKED ABOUT GROWING UP on a ranch in West Texas, my mother often recounts an early childhood memory of my grandmother, outfitted in a long dress, bonnet, and work gloves, killing a rattlesnake with a hoe in her orchard behind their house. Even when my grandparents left the ranch and moved to town, my grandmother still kept peach and apricot trees in a small orchard behind the house. I can still picture her sitting on the porch with a wooden-handled paring knife and an apron full of peaches, removing the stones and cutting the fruit into a white porcelain bowl for pies, cobblers, and preserves.

She also grew grapes—small, somewhat sour clusters that we would snack on from the vine—that she would turn into grape pies. One of her neighbors had wild blackberry bushes. Once a year she would drag my brother and me along to pick buckets full of berries from the thorny bushes with the promise of a cobbler with ice cream.

The most common dessert in my grandmother's kitchen was pound cake. She made the classic loaf pan version that was buttery and moist. She would serve it as an afternoon snack, or, for dessert, she would lightly toast a fat slice in butter and top it with peach preserves and whipped cream.

Though my mother is not a great baker, she learned from her mother how to bake a pound cake. Chocolate fudge, lemon poppy seed, cornmeal almond, banana nut, and cinnamon coffee cake all appeared in our kitchen, all made using slight variations on the basic pound cake method.

To this day, my mother doesn't understand the science of baking, such as why and how each ingredient works. She does, however, know that if you follow the directions for pound cake that are written in the margins of an old tattered Helen Corbitt cookbook, you will end up with something tasty for dessert.

Along the way to becoming a working chef, I've learned that more than being able to read a recipe, it's important to know why a recipe does or doesn't work, and this is more critical in baking than in any other type of cooking. Baking is much more of a science than it is an art. In fact, in baking, recipes are often referred to as "formulas." In order to understand how a formula works, you need to know how the different ingredients used in baking function.

For easy family desserts, try the Lemon Pound Cake (page 227), Lambert's Fudge Brownies (page 224), or the Carmelita Bars (page 216). When you're having a group over for dinner, a big Peach Cake Cobbler (page 228) or Maple Bread Pudding (page 225) is hard to beat. And when I want to treat myself, I'll make Gingered Pear Fried Pies (page 221), a big Buttermilk Chocolate Cake (page 214), or Mexican Flan (page 219).

Buttermilk-Honey Ice Cream

The buttermilk and lemon in this ice cream impart just the right amount of tartness, which is perfect alongside summer fruit and berry cobblers and pies.

MAKES 1¹/₂ QUARTS

2 cups heavy cream

¹/₂ cup honey

¹/₂ cup sugar

¹/₄ teaspoon salt

2 egg yolks

2 cups buttermilk

Juice and zest of 1 lemon

1 teaspoon vanilla extract

In a medium saucepan, combine 1¹/₂ cups of the cream with the honey and bring to a simmer.

Meanwhile, in a mixing bowl, whisk together the sugar and salt with the remaining ¹/₂ cup cream and the egg yolks. When the cream and honey mixture reaches a simmer, remove it from the heat. Temper the egg yolk mixture by adding the hot cream mixture, a little bit at a time, whisking constantly, until the egg yolk mixture is warm. Now add the warmed egg yolk mixture back to the saucepan with the remaining hot cream, whisking to incorporate. Return the saucepan to the stove over medium heat, stirring constantly, until it returns to a simmer, and slowly bring the mixture back to a simmer, cooking for another minute until the cream has thickened. Remove from the heat.

Add the buttermilk, lemon juice and zest, and vanilla to the cream mixture and whisk to combine. Transfer the custard to a large bowl, cover with plastic wrap, and refrigerate until completely cool, about 1 hour.

Transfer the chilled custard to your ice cream-maker and follow the manufacturer's directions to churn into ice cream.

Buttermilk Chocolate Cake

A restaurant serving bold dishes of grilled and smoked meats needs to have a stellar chocolate dessert on the menu. Years ago I asked our pastry chef, James Smith, to come up with a rich chocolate cake that was powerful enough to be on the menu at Lambert's. He gave me one of his "I'm too busy today to humor you" looks, but later that afternoon he left a buttermilk chocolate cake in the kitchen. He had re-created his grandmother's cake that he remembered from his childhood. The crumb was rich and dense, with the sweetness of the chocolate balanced by the slight sourness of the buttermilk. The icing was cooked fudge, giving the cake a second punch of chocolate and a creamy mouthfeel. From that day on, we have had James's cake on the menu. It's a great way to finish a meal, but it's also great with a glass of milk before bed.

MAKES 8 TO 10 SERVINGS

3 cups all-purpose flour

1 cup unsweetened natural or Dutch-processed cocoa powder

1¹/₂ teaspoons baking soda

1¹/₂ teaspoons baking powder

¹/₄ teaspoon salt

1¹/₂ cups unsalted butter, at room temperature

1¹/₂ cups sugar

4 eggs

2³/₄ cups buttermilk

1 tablespoon vanilla extract

Chocolate Fudge Icing (page 215)

Preheat your oven to 350°F. Grease two 9-inch round cake pans and line each with parchment paper.

In a bowl, sift together the flour, cocoa powder, baking soda, baking powder, and salt and set aside.

Add the butter and sugar to the bowl of your stand mixer with the paddle attachment, and cream the mixture on high speed until the butter is light and fluffy, about 3 minutes. Add the eggs one at a time, beating thoroughly after each addition.

In a small bowl, stir together the buttermilk and vanilla. Add half the dry ingredients and half of the buttermilk mixture to the butter mixture and briefly mix on low speed for 15 seconds. Scrape down the bowl and add the remaining dry and wet ingredients. Mix on low just until the batter comes together, about 30 seconds. You may have to finish mixing the batter with a rubber spatula to combine all the ingredients, but avoid overmixing the batter or you will end up with a flat, dense cake.

Transfer the batter to the prepared cake pans and bake until a toothpick inserted in the middle of the cake comes out clean, 35 to 40 minutes. Allow the cakes to cool in the pans for about 5 minutes before turning out onto wire racks and letting them cool completely.

Frost the layers with the Chocolate Fudge Icing and serve.

CHOCOLATE FUDGE ICING

FROSTS ONE 9-INCH LAYER CAKE

2 cups sugar

1 (12-ounce) can
evaporated milk

8 ounces unsweetened
chocolate

1¹/₂ teaspoons vanilla
extract

1¹/₂ cups cubed
unsalted butter, at
room temperature

Combine the sugar and evaporated milk in a saucepan and bring to a boil. Continue to boil for exactly 7 minutes. Remove from the heat and set aside.

Place the chocolate in a stainless steel bowl over a pot of simmering water or in the top of a double boiler and melt the chocolate, stirring frequently. Stir the chocolate into the hot milk and sugar mixture.

Add the vanilla and butter to the chocolate mixture adding a few pieces of butter at a time, whisking to incorporate until smooth. Allow the icing to rest, cooling, for 5 minutes before frosting the cake.

[Science of Baking, part 1]

Flour is the main ingredient, by volume, of almost all bread and pastry products; it is what gives structure and body to baked goods. Broadly speaking, flour is a powder made of cereal or nut grains, but flour made from wheat is by far the most commonly used and is one of the most important foods in the American diet. Flour, though, can also be made from corn, rye, potatoes, rice, roots, fruit, nuts, buckwheat, and soybeans, to name just a few ingredients.

Wheat flour is available in several different forms. Most of the flour and baked products we see in the store are made from white flour, which has had the wheat grain's bran and germ removed. Whole grain flour, on the other hand, is made by grinding the entire grain—endosperm, germ, and bran—as the name suggests.

Most commercial bakeries use two types of white flour: **bread flour** (also known as **hard flour**), which has a high gluten content and gives bread its shape and firm texture, and **cake flour** (also known as **soft flour**), which is low in gluten and gives cakes and pastries a more delicate texture. When making pastries and quick breads, bakers will sometimes combine bread and cake flours to achieve the texture they are looking for in the finished baked good. A pastry that needs to hold its shape and have some structure, such as a croissant, will often contain a little more bread flour than cake flour. However, quick breads such as muffins will tend to be made with a little more cake flour so that the finished product will be light and tender. All-purpose flour, which has a gluten level in between that of bread flour and cake flour, is most often used by home cooks since it will work in most recipes.

Carmelita Bars

This recipe was originally created for a holiday party we catered for Lady Bird Johnson at the ranch. It's the perfect bar cookie, with chewy oats and carmel, chocolate chips, and walnuts. We serve it at the restaurant warmed through, topped with vanilla ice cream and a rich caramel sauce.

MAKES 48 BARS

2 cups vegetable shortening

1 cup unsalted butter, at room temperature

6 cups quick oats (not instant or old-fashioned)

3 cups firmly packed brown sugar

2 cups whole wheat flour

2 teaspoons baking soda

1 teaspoon cinnamon

1 teaspoon salt

3 cups semisweet chocolate chips

3 cups chopped walnuts

4 cups purchased caramel topping

3/4 cup all-purpose flour

Preheat your oven to 350°F. Coat the bottom and sides of a 12 by 17-inch baking pan with nonstick vegetable oil spray. Line the bottom of the pan with parchment paper. Coat the parchment with more of the vegetable oil spray.

Combine the shortening, butter, oats, brown sugar, flour, baking soda, cinnamon, and salt in the bowl of your stand mixer. Mix with the paddle attachment on slow speed until chunky crumbs form, about 3 minutes. Set aside half of the mixture, and press the remaining half into an even layer in the prepared baking pan. Bake for 12 minutes.

Remove the pan from the oven and sprinkle the chocolate chips and walnuts over the top of prebaked crumb mixture. In a bowl, stir together the caramel topping and flour. Drizzle the mixture over the chocolate chips and walnuts. Sprinkle the remaining crumb mixture evenly over the top of the caramel.

Return the pan to the oven and bake until the top is golden brown, 20 to 25 minutes. Remove the pan from the oven, run a spatula around edge of pan, and place on a wire rack to cool. When completely cool, cut into 2 by 2-inch squares to serve.

Chocolate Mocha Ice Cream

My father loved to make ice cream when I was a kid. In the summer, when the barbecue pit was loaded with steaks or smoked meats, he would always make a batch of ice cream to finish the meal. This is one of my favorite ice creams, and it's great at the end of a big steak dinner. The rich chocolate is balanced with just the right amount of espresso.

MAKES 1½ QUARTS

2 cups heavy cream

1 cup sugar

¼ teaspoon salt

2 egg yolks

2 ounces semisweet chocolate chips

½ cup espresso, freshly brewed or instant

2 teaspoons vanilla extract

2 cups half-and-half

In a medium saucepan, bring 1½ cups of the cream to a simmer.

Meanwhile, in a mixing bowl, whisk together the sugar and salt. Whisk in the remaining ½ cup cream and the egg yolks.

When the cream reaches a simmer, remove it from the heat. Temper the egg yolk mixture by slowly adding the hot cream, a little bit at a time, whisking constantly, until the egg yolk mixture is warm. Now add the warmed egg yolk mixture back to the saucepan with the remaining hot cream, whisking to incorporate. Return the saucepan to the stove over medium heat, stirring constantly, until it returns to a simmer, and slowly bring the mixture back to a simmer, cooking for another minute until the cream has thickened. Remove from the heat.

Stir the chocolate chips into the hot cream mixture until the chocolate has completely melted. Add the espresso, vanilla, and half-and-half and whisk to combine. Transfer the custard to a large bowl, cover with plastic wrap, and refrigerate until completely cool.

Transfer the chilled custard to your ice cream maker and follow the manufacturer's directions to churn into ice cream.

Mexican Flan

The Italians have panna cotta and the French have crème brûlée, but my favorite creamy dessert is a well-executed Mexican flan. During baking, the caramel in the bottom of the ramekins turns into a sweet and slightly bitter sauce for these light and creamy flans. For a buffet, you can make a large flan by using a loaf pan instead of individual ramekins.

MAKES 8 SERVINGS

³/₄ cup sugar

1 (14-ounce) can sweetened condensed milk

2 cups heavy cream

1 cup milk

4 eggs

1 egg yolk

2 teaspoons vanilla extract

Sweetened whipped cream, for garnish

¹/₂ pint fresh berries, for garnish

Preheat your oven to 350°F.

In a small nonstick saucepan, heat the sugar over medium-low heat, swirling the pan occasionally so that it melts evenly. Cook the sugar until it is melted and golden brown, about 5 minutes. Divide the caramel evenly among eight 6-ounce ramekins. Set aside.

In a bowl, stir together the sweetened condensed milk, cream, and milk. In another bowl, whisk together the eggs, egg yolk, and vanilla. Gradually whisk the milk mixture into the egg mixture, being careful not to incorporate too much air. Pour the custard through a fine-mesh sieve into the ramekins. Place the ramekins in a deep baking dish and place in the oven. Carefully add about 1 inch of hot water to the baking dish to create a water bath. Bake until the flans' centers are set, about 50 minutes.

Remove the ramekins from the water bath and transfer to a wire rack. Let cool at room temperature for about 30 minutes and then cover and transfer to the refrigerator until ready to serve.

To serve, run a sharp knife carefully around the edge of each flan and then dip the bottom of each ramekin in a bowl of hot water to loosen the caramel. Turn the ramekin over your serving plate and unmold, allowing the caramel to drip on top of and around the flan. Garnish with a dollop of whipped cream and a few fresh berries.

Gingered Pear Fried Pies

Fried pies originated, so the story goes, when cooks would use leftover pie dough and filling to make little fried treats for the kids hanging around the kitchen. However they came to pass, fried pies are such a mainstay in the South that you can buy them at the cash register in most gas stations. When I wanted to put a fried pie on the menu at the restaurant, James Smith came up with something like a beignet or doughnut dough, adding a little candied ginger to the vanilla-flavored pears to fancy it up a bit. Try this recipe with the gingered pears, or use your favorite pie filling. Either way, it makes a great treat in your kid's lunch box or a dessert served warm from the fryer with a scoop of Buttermilk-Honey Ice Cream (page 213).

MAKES 16 FRIED PIES

DOUGH

2 cups unsalted butter

1/2 cup sugar

4 eggs

5 cups all-purpose flour

2 teaspoons baking powder

2 teaspoons salt

PEAR FILLING

8 medium-size pears, Comice or other firm, ripe variety, peeled, cored, cut into 1/2-inch dice

1 1/2 cups sugar

1 tablespoon vanilla extract

1/2 cup finely diced crystallized ginger

2 tablespoons unsalted butter

2 tablespoons cornstarch

1/4 cup apple juice

1 egg

1 tablespoon water

Pinch of salt

Vegetable oil, for frying

Powdered sugar, for dusting

In the bowl of your stand mixer using the paddle attachment, cream the butter and sugar on medium-high speed until light and fluffy, about 5 minutes. Scrape the bowl down and add the eggs one at a time, mixing well after each addition.

In a separate bowl, sift together the flour, baking powder, and salt. Add half of the flour mixture to the butter mixture and mix slowly just until incorporated. Add the second half of the flour mixture to the butter mixture and continue mixing until a soft dough has formed. Wrap the dough in plastic and chill in the refrigerator for 1 hour.

Meanwhile, in a large sauté pan, combine the pears, sugar, vanilla, ginger, and butter and cook over medium-high heat until the pears have softened, about 4 minutes. Meanwhile, make a slurry by mixing together the cornstarch and apple juice in a small bowl. Add the slurry to the pear mixture and cook until the liquid has thickened and become clear, about 1 minute. Transfer the pear mixture to a bowl, cover, and chill in the refrigerator for at least 30 minutes before forming the pies.

Before assembling the pies, make the egg wash by whisking together egg, water, and salt in a small bowl.

When you are ready to assemble your pies, divide dough into fourths. On a lightly floured work surface, roll one section of the dough out to a thickness of 1/8 inch and cut into sixteen 8-inch rounds. Place about 1/2 cup of the pear filling in the center of each round. Brush the edges of the dough with egg wash, fold in half, and press the tines of a fork along the edges to seal.

(continued on next page)

(Gingered Pear Fried Pies, continued)

Repeat with the remaining sections of dough. Refrigerate the assembled pies for 1 hour to chill through.

To fry the pies, fill a large, deep skillet with the vegetable oil to a depth of 3 inches and heat to 350°F. Carefully add a few of the pies and fry until they are golden brown and the dough is cooked all the way through, about 3 minutes per side. Transfer the fried pies to a plate lined with paper towels to drain. Dust with powdered sugar just before serving, either warm or at room temperature.

[Science of Baking, part 2]

Butter is made by churning fresh or fermented cream or milk. Butter consists of butterfat, water, and milk proteins. In the United States, commercial butter is about 80 percent butterfat and 15 percent water. European butter generally has a higher ratio of butterfat, about 85 percent.

In the past, on family farms, milk would typically be gathered for a few days before it was churned and turned into butter. As the milk slightly fermented or soured, bacteria would turn the milk sugars into lactic acid, which would give the finished butter a fuller, richer flavor. Butter made from fermented milk is known as cultured butter. Today, modern dairies make cultured butter by first pasteurizing the cream and then adding bacteria for fermentation.

When fresh cream is pasteurized and made into butter without fermentation, it is labeled as sweet cream butter. Butter made from fresh or cultured unpasteurized cream is called raw cream butter and has a cleaner cream flavor. Cultured butter is preferred throughout continental Europe, while sweet cream butter is dominant in the United States and Great Britain. Because of this, cultured butter is sometimes labeled "European butter" when it is sold in the United States.

Normally, butter softens enough to be "spreadable" at around 60°F, well above refrigerated temperature. Manufacturers have developed several butter products that are soft and spreadable directly from the refrigerator by chemically manipulating it and by adding different oils. Whipped butter, for example, is made by incorporating nitrogen gas into the butter.

All of these different types of butter are sold either salted or unsalted. Salt, which enhances the flavor and acts as a preservative, may be added to the butter during processing either in a granulated form or as a salty brine. At my restaurants, we never use salted butter when we're baking because we want to control the amount of salt we add to our recipes. The only time we use salted butter is to serve with the bread at the table.

Butter serves several important roles in baking. Butter gives baked goods both flavor and a smooth mouthfeel. Just as important, butter acts as a leavening agent in many baked products. In pie dough and pastries, for example, the butter solids, when heated during baking, release water in the form of steam, creating air pockets and thus a flaky dough. In quick breads and cakes, the butter is whipped, incorporating air into the batter. The water in the butter, again in the form of steam, leavens the batter during baking, creating a light and airy crumb.

Lambert's Fudge Brownies

Years ago a team from Lambert's went in search of the perfect brownie. After weeks of testing and eating them, we finally settled on this recipe as our house brownie. We sell these at Jo's Coffee Shop and do an à la mode version with vanilla ice cream and chocolate sauce at Lambert's. The finished brownie is like the perfect fudge cake with a matte crisp crust. If you're not a fan of pecans, you can substitute walnuts, or just skip the nuts altogether.

MAKES 16 BROWNIES

2½ cups semisweet chocolate chips, divided use

3 cups canola oil

2 cups firmly packed brown sugar

4 eggs

2 teaspoons vanilla extract

1⅓ cups all-purpose flour

1 teaspoon baking soda

½ cup unsweetened natural or Dutch processed cocoa powder

3 cups pecans

Preheat your oven to 350°F. Coat a 9 by 13-inch baking dish with nonstick vegetable oil spray.

In a stainless steel bowl over a pot of simmering water or in the top of a double boiler, melt 1½ cups of chocolate chips, stirring frequently, until completely smooth. Set aside.

In a large bowl, combine the oil, brown sugar, eggs, and vanilla and whisk until smooth. Then add the melted chocolate and whisk until combined.

In a separate bowl, sift together the flour, baking soda, and cocoa. Add the dry ingredients to the wet ingredients and, using a rubber spatula or spoon, stir until all the dry ingredients are moistened. Stir in the remaining 1 cup chocolate chips and the pecans.

Spread the batter in the prepared baking dish and bake until the center is set, 50 minutes to 1 hour. Allow to cool in the pan for about 30 minutes, then transfer to a wire rack to finish cooling before cutting into 16 squares and serving.

Maple Bread Pudding

Maple brioche bread pudding has been our signature dessert at Lambert's for years. We have refined a standard bread pudding by using rich brioche, maple syrup, and a richer custard to bind everything together.

MAKES 10 TO 12 SERVINGS

1 loaf brioche, cut into 2-inch cubes

4 tablespoons unsalted butter, melted

1½ cups egg yolks (from about 18 eggs)

½ cup sugar

1 teaspoon ground cinnamon

½ teaspoon freshly grated nutmeg

1½ cups maple syrup

2 cups heavy cream

1 teaspoon vanilla extract

½ teaspoon salt

Maple Bourbon Hard Sauce (see recipe), for serving

Preheat your oven to 400°F. Toss the bread cubes in the melted butter, place in a single layer on a baking sheet, and toast in the oven until evenly golden brown, about 12 minutes. Remove the bread from the oven and turn the heat down to 350°F.

In a large bowl, whisk together the egg yolks, sugar, cinnamon, nutmeg, maple syrup, cream, vanilla, and salt. Add the toasted bread and let soak for 20 minutes.

Transfer the bread custard to a deep 9 by 13-inch baking dish. Place the baking dish in a larger pan and fill the pan with enough hot water to come halfway up the sides of the custard dish. Carefully place the custard in its water bath into the oven and bake until the custard is set and evenly browned on top, 45 minutes to 1 hour.

Transfer to a wire rack and let cool for at least 30 minutes before serving. Serve warm. Top each serving with a big spoonful of the hard sauce. To reheat any leftover bread pudding, cover with foil and place in a 250°F oven until warmed through.

MAPLE-BOURBON HARD SAUCE

MAKES ABOUT 3 CUPS

1½ cups maple syrup

¼ cup firmly packed brown sugar

⅓ cup unsalted butter

⅓ cup bourbon

Juice of ¼ lemon (1 teaspoon)

In a small saucepan, bring the maple syrup and brown sugar to a boil. Reduce the heat to a simmer and whisk in the butter until melted and thoroughly incorporated. Remove the saucepan from heat and stir in the bourbon and lemon juice.

Lemon Pound Cake

This is the dessert of my childhood because it's what my mother made most often. My grandmother, a great baker, would always have a pound cake around the kitchen. She would serve it for breakfast or as a simple dessert topped with fresh berries or apricots and peaches she had put up from her orchard. This recipe works best if all the ingredients are at room temperature.

MAKES 1 LOAF, SERVING 8 TO 10

11 tablespoons unsalted butter, at room temperature

²/₃ cups vegetable shortening

2¹/₄ cups sugar

4 eggs, at room temperature

3 cups sifted all-purpose flour

¹/₂ teaspoon salt

¹/₂ teaspoon baking soda

1 cup buttermilk, at room temperature

1¹/₂ teaspoons vanilla extract

2 tablespoons fresh lemon juice

Preheat your oven to 325°F. Grease a 9 by 5-inch loaf pan and line the bottom with parchment paper.

Combine the butter, shortening, and sugar in the bowl of your stand mixer and, using the paddle attachment, cream until light and fluffy at high speed, stopping to scrape down the sides as necessary. Turn the mixer to medium and add the eggs one at a time, mixing thoroughly after each addition.

In a small bowl, whisk together the flour, salt, and baking soda. In another small bowl, stir together the buttermilk, vanilla, and lemon juice.

Add half of the flour mixture and half of the buttermilk mixture to the creamed butter and eggs. Mix on low speed until just incorporated. Add the remaining flour and buttermilk mixtures and continue to mix until the batter just comes together. Pour the batter into the prepared loaf pan, lightly tapping the pan on your countertop to release any air pockets. Place in the oven and bake until a toothpick inserted in the middle of the loaf comes out clean, about 1 hour and 15 minutes. Transfer to a wire rack and allow the cake to cool in the pan for about 20 minutes before turning it out to finish cooling.

Peach Cake Cobbler

There are two types of cobbler in this world: cake cobbler and pie cobbler. To me, there should be no debate—and no pie cobbler. A pie cobbler is nothing but an attempt to bake a pie without taking the time to make a bottom crust. A cake cobbler, on the other hand, gives you layers of sweet gooey fruit dispersed amidst a light, moist cake. What more needs to be said? This simple cake cobbler recipe also works great with apples and pears. When substituting berries, there's no need to precook the fruit. Just toss the berries in the brown sugar and add them to the melted butter before topping with the cobbler dough.

MAKES 8 TO 10 SERVINGS

½ cup unsalted butter

8 cups peeled, pitted, and sliced fresh peaches

¾ cup firmly packed brown sugar

2¼ cups all-purpose flour

1½ cups plus 3 tablespoons sugar

2¼ teaspoons baking powder

½ teaspoon salt

1½ teaspoons ground cinnamon

2¼ cups milk

¼ cup buttermilk

2 teaspoons vanilla extract

Whipped cream or vanilla ice cream, for serving

Preheat your oven to 375°F.

Melt the butter in a 9 by 13-inch baking dish in the oven. In a large bowl, toss the peaches with the brown sugar to coat and then arrange the peaches in an even layer in the melted butter. Return the dish to the oven until the peaches begin to soften and start releasing some of their juice, 10 to 15 minutes.

Meanwhile, sift the flour, 1½ cups of sugar, the baking powder, salt, and cinnamon into a large bowl. Add the milk, buttermilk, and vanilla to the dry ingredients and stir until smooth. Pour the batter evenly over the fruit. Sprinkle with the remaining 3 tablespoons of sugar.

Bake the cobbler until the center is beginning to brown and is set, 50 minutes to 1 hour. Serve warm with a big dollop of whipped cream or a scoop of vanilla ice cream.

[Science of Baking, part 3]

To most people, sugar is just that sweet white crystalline stuff you put in your iced tea or coffee, but it's a little more complex than that. Sugar, whose main forms are sucrose, lactose, and fructose, is a basic food carbohydrate. It primarily comes from sugarcane and sugar beets, but it also is found in fruit, honey, sorghum, sugar maple, and many other sources.

The majority of refined white sugar used in the United States today comes from sugarcane or sugar beets, and there is little difference between the two. Cane sugar is made by extracting the juice from the cane and then filtering and boiling the juices to produce sugar crystals. Beet sugar is produced by boiling the beets in hot water and using controlled crystallization to extract the sugars.

Granulated white sugar comes in various crystal sizes:

- Coarse-grained sugars, often labeled as sugar nibs or sanding sugar, are used for decorating baked goods. The large size of the crystal makes this size perfect for giving baked goods a shiny finish.

- Normal granulated table sugar is the most common grain size.

- Finer-grained sugars are the result of selectively sieving granulated sugar. There's superfine sugar, used for flavoring drinks or making meringues, and powdered sugar, confectioners' sugar, or 10X sugar, the finest grade and used for baking and dusting.

- Brown sugar comes from the later stages of sugar refining, when sugar forms crystals with significant molasses content, or by coating white refined sugar with cane molasses syrup. The darker the brown sugar, the higher the moisture content and molasses flavor.

Roasted Peanut and Peanut Butter Cookies

This is the best-selling cookie at our coffee shop, Jo's, in Austin. The cookie has a little crunch while the center remains moist. The roasted peanuts give these cookies just the right amount of saltiness.

MAKES 20 COOKIES

1 cup unsalted butter, at room temperature

1³/₄ cups firmly packed brown sugar

2 cups creamy peanut butter

2 eggs

2 teaspoons vanilla extract

2¹/₄ cups all-purpose flour

1 teaspoon baking soda

¹/₄ teaspoon ground cinnamon

2 cups dry roasted peanuts

Preheat your oven to 350°F. Line a baking sheet with parchment paper.

In the bowl of a stand mixer using the paddle attachment, cream the butter and brown sugar on medium speed until fluffy. Scrape the bowl down and add the peanut butter. Return the mixer to medium speed and mix until the dough is thoroughly combined. Turn the mixer to low and add the eggs one at a time, mixing thoroughly after each addition. Add the vanilla and continue mixing until incorporated.

In a separate bowl, sift together the flour, baking soda, and cinnamon. Add the flour mixture to the creamed mixture, then mix on low speed until just combined. Remove the bowl from the mixer and fold in the peanuts with a rubber spatula.

Divide the dough into 20 balls of equal size and place on the prepared baking sheet about 3 inches apart. Using the back of a fork, push down on each ball to flatten it to about ¹/₂ inch thick. Bake until the cookies start to brown on the edges, about 15 to 20 minutes. Transfer the cookies to a wire rack to cool. Once the cookies are cool, store them in an airtight container.

Tres Leches Cake

Tres leches (Spanish for "three milks") is a favorite at Mexican restaurants and often served on special occasions. The rich cake becomes moist and dense when it is soaked in a syrup made from three types of milk. And, as though it weren't quite rich enough, it is then topped with whipped cream and garnished with chocolate and fresh berries.

MAKES 12 SERVINGS

2¼ cups all-purpose flour

1½ teaspoons baking powder

¾ teaspoon salt

¾ cup unsalted butter, at room temperature

1½ cups sugar

6 eggs

2¼ teaspoons vanilla extract

1 cup milk

3 cups heavy cream

1 (14-ounce) can sweetened condensed milk

¼ cup powdered sugar

¼ cup chocolate shavings

½ pint fresh berries, for garnish

Preheat your oven to 350°F. Lightly grease and flour a 9 by 13-inch baking dish.

In a bowl, sift together the flour, baking powder, and salt.

Using your stand mixer with the paddle attachment, cream the butter and sugar together at medium speed until light and fluffy. Reduce the mixer speed to low and add the eggs one at a time, mixing thoroughly after each addition. Mix in 1¼ teaspoons of the vanilla. Next add the flour mixture in 3 increments, mixing on low after each addition until just until combined.

Spread the batter in the prepared baking dish and bake until it begins to brown and a toothpick inserted in the center comes out clean, 20 to 25 minutes.

Let the cake cool on a wire rack until it comes to room temperature. Transfer the cake to a serving platter. Poke holes, about and 2 inches apart, all the way to the bottom of the cake by inserting a skewer or dinner fork. Cover and refrigerate the cake for 30 minutes.

In a bowl, whisk together the milk, 1 cup of the cream, and the sweetened condensed milk until combined. Remove the cake from the refrigerator and slowly pour the milk mixture over the cake. Return to the refrigerator for at least 1 hour, or up to overnight. Occasionally spoon the glaze that has run off back onto the cake.

In the bowl of a stand mixer with the whisk attachment, combine the remaining 2 cups cream, the powdered sugar, and the remaining 1 teaspoon vanilla until stiff peaks form. Spread a thin layer over the soaked cake and then sprinkle the cake with the chocolate shavings. Cut the cake into 12 squares, each about 3 by 3 inches square, and serve each piece garnished with a few fresh berries.

WHEN A RECIPE CALLS FOR CHOCOLATE SHAVINGS, I like to make them with bittersweet chocolate bars or chips. Whichever you use, make sure the chocolate is cold when working with it. To make shavings from a bar, use a vegetable peeler to shave off thin strips. If you are using chocolate chips, place the cold chips in a food processor and pulse the machine a few times to break them up. Don't overprocess the chips or you will end up with chocolate syrup. Store the chocolate shavings in an airtight container in your refrigerator for use in baking, or just sprinkle them over a bowl of ice cream, like I do.

[Science of Baking, part 4]

Most quick breads and cake batters contain eggs. There are a few different types of eggs available in specialty markets today, but here we are only going to be concerned with the chicken egg, which is by far the most commonly used.

Most chicken eggs sold in the United States are white. We are seeing more brown eggs in specialty stores today, but the truth is that brown eggs taste exactly like white ones and, nutritionally, are no better or worse for you.

The major factor influencing an egg's flavor is the feed that the chicken eats. Some folks think that free-range chickens taste better and are better for you, but the truth is that the unpredictable diet of a free-range chicken will produce unpredictably flavored eggs. Some folks feel that eggs are better when a rooster is allowed to do as he pleases with the hens. Again, this does not influence the egg's flavor. And a fertilized egg that has been refrigerated tastes no different than an unfertilized egg, since the cold temperature prohibits cellular growth.

The egg is made up of the yolk and the white. Unscientifically speaking, the yolk is basically fat and the white is primarily protein and water. This is important for us to understand when using eggs in baking.

Since the yolk is mostly fat, it carries most of the egg's flavor. Egg yolks are used for emulsifying and adding richness to sauces and dressings, as well as to thicken puddings and custards. In baking, yolks give richness and body to quick breads and cakes.

Egg whites are also widely used in kitchen. When separated from the yolk, the whites can be whipped to form light and fluffy meringues and mousses, and to add body and volume to baked goods. In quick breads and cakes, in which whole eggs are typically used, the protein in the egg white coagulates during cooking and gives structure to the leavening caused by steam from the butter and the rise from the baking soda and powder.

The pound cake is the simplest of desserts, with only four key ingredients. Each of the ingredients has its own specific role in making the pound cake work. The flour provides the main structure and volume of the cake. The butter gives you the flavor, a creamy mouthfeel, and moisture, and it helps aerate and leaven the cake. The sugar sweetens the whole thing while providing a little moisture and structure. The eggs do double duty by providing creaminess and body with the yolk and structure from the white.

Now that you understand the science of a pound cake, get back in the kitchen and have some fun. Change things up and make it your own.

STOCKS & SAUCES

IN BIG COMMERCIAL KITCHENS there are cooks whose only job is to make stocks and sauces eight to ten hours a day. They are at the ovens roasting bones and at the stoves reaching into twenty-gallon stockpots, skimming, reducing, and tasting. My first job in a big city kitchen was as a hot prep cook at Postrio in San Francisco. My primary responsibility was to produce stocks—brown veal, chicken, duck, lamb, fish, lobster, and game stocks—to be used by the line cooks. I quickly learned that the quality of all the sauces that were eaten at the restaurant was dependent on the quality of the stocks that I produced. The same holds true in my kitchens today, both at home and at the restaurant. No matter how skilled a cook you are, your sauces are only going to taste as good as the ingredients that go into them.

A sauce's sole purpose is to support the food that it is being served with. A simple brown beef sauce with mushrooms complements the rich flavors of a slow-roasted prime rib. Other sauces act more as condiments with contrasting flavors—fruited mustard with a smoked pork chop or a vinegary chimichurri with a grilled beef rib eye. For me, a well-prepared sauce will accomplish a little of both, complementing and extending the flavors of a dish while imparting enough contrast to highlight its unique characteristics.

The backbone of a lot of soups and sauces is a quality stock. Making a stock can be as simple as simmering bones with vegetables, as when combining chicken bones, onion, carrot, and celery. For more depth in a stock, the bones can be roasted until caramelized and then cooked with wine, tomatoes, herbs, and spices. Stocks can be light and subtle, like a clear fish stock used in a soup, or they can be bold and flavorful, like a shrimp stock for a gumbo or Creole sauce.

Here I've included a couple of recipes for barbecue sauces and salsas—for us, the workhorses of the restaurant. You can adjust the tartness and sweetness of the barbecue sauces and the heat of the salsas to your taste or according to their intended use. A rich Texas barbecue sauce is perfect with a smoked beef brisket, whereas a spicy vinegar sauce works great with fatty pork butt. A hot chile pepper sauce is used as a condiment to add a touch of spice to a meal, and a green or red salsa is for munching with chips and slathering on a plate of enchiladas.

Don't let the French names make you nervous. The most important things to remember when making stocks and sauces is to use the proper technique and to learn the way ingredients work together to build flavors and structure.

What Is a Roux?

A proper roux is made with three parts flour to two parts fat. Clarified butter is the fat most commonly used in professional kitchens, but a vegetable or animal fat is just fine. I usually try to use fat that is complementary to the sauce I am making (butter for a cream sauce or animal fat for a meat sauce). The fat is heated in a pan over medium heat and the flour is stirred in and cooked to give the flour a slightly nutty flavor.

There are three basic types of roux:

A **white roux** is cooked for only a couple of minutes and is barely colored, so it is perfect for making white sauces. A **blond roux** is cooked a little longer, until it develops a light straw color and a more pronounced nutty flavor. **Brown roux**, which is cooked to a deep brown color and has a pronounced nutty flavor, is used primarily in Creole and Cajun cooking. The longer and darker you cook a roux, the more the starch in the flour breaks down, and thus the less thickening power the roux has.

In general, a roux and liquid should be combined in one of two ways. A cool roux may be added to a hot liquid, or a hot roux can be added to a cool liquid. Once the roux has been added to the liquid, cook the sauce at a low simmer for at least 15 minutes to cook out the raw taste of the flour.

Brown Beef Stock

The quality of a brown beef stock is dependent on the bones used to prepare it. Knuckle or neck bones are preferred, as these joint bones contain more collagen, which produces a richer and more gelatinous stock. It is the gelatin in the joints that gives the stock a velvety mouthfeel and helps to thicken it as it reduces. A lot of chefs use veal knuckles for a brown stock because of the large amount of gelatin in their bones (and their shorter cooking time). Don't be afraid to roast the bones and mirepoix to a dark, dark brown; it will give you the flavor and color necessary for a great stock.

MAKES 1 GALLON

¼ cup vegetable oil

8 pounds beef knuckle or neck bones

1 large yellow onion, coarsely diced

2 carrots, peeled and coarsely chopped

2 stalks celery, coarsely chopped

3 tablespoons tomato paste

1 cup dry red wine

6 quarts water

2 bay leaves

¼ bunch fresh thyme

½ bunch flat-leaf parsley

1 teaspoon black peppercorns

1 teaspoon kosher salt

Preheat your oven to 425°F. Coat the bottom of a roasting pan large enough to hold the bones in a single layer with the vegetable oil. Place the pan in the oven to preheat for about 15 minutes. Add the bones to the pan in a single layer and roast, turning occasionally, until the bones are an even dark brown, about 45 minutes.

With a pair of tongs, transfer the bones to a large stockpot, leaving the fat and drippings behind in the roasting pan. Carefully add the vegetables to the pan in a single layer and return the pan to the oven. As you did the bones, roast the vegetables, stirring occasionally, until they are a dark brown, about 30 minutes.

Add the tomato paste to the vegetables, stirring to combine. Return the vegetables to the oven and continue to cook for another 15 minutes. The vegetables and tomato paste will become very dark and start to stick to the bottom of the pan. Remove from the oven and transfer the vegetables to the stockpot with the bones.

Place the roasting pan on your stove over medium-high heat. Add the wine and 2 cups of the water to the pan and deglaze, scraping the bottom of the pan to release any of the crusty fond (brown bits). Add the deglazing liquid to the stockpot along with the remaining 5 quarts and 2 cups of water. Bring the stock to a simmer and skim off any fat or scum that floats to the top with a ladle. Cook the stock at a low simmer for 5 hours, continuing to skim the surface.

After 5 hours, add the bay leaves, thyme, parsley, peppercorns, and salt. Continue to cook at a low simmer for 3 hours more. After 8 hours total, strain through a colander. Cool down quickly in an ice bath or in a shallow pan in the refrigerator.

Chicken Stock

Whenever I am breaking down chickens at home, I save all the bones in a bag and freeze them. When I get about 8 to 10 pounds built up in the freezer, I'll make a batch of chicken stock. I'll whack up the chicken bones into 3-inch pieces with a meat cleaver—the more surface area, the more flavor the bones can release. Most chicken stocks, like this one, are clear. If the color of the finished stock is not a concern in the recipe I am making, I prefer a roasted chicken stock, which has more flavor. To make a roasted chicken stock, follow the procedure for roasting the bones and mirepoix in the Brown Beef Stock recipe (page 237), adding a tablespoon of tomato paste to the mirepoix at the end of roasting.

MAKES 1 GALLON

8 pounds chicken bones

1 large yellow onion, medium diced

2 carrots, medium diced

2 stalks celery, medium diced

2 bay leaves

½ bunch flat-leaf parsley

¼ bunch fresh thyme

1 teaspoon black peppercorns

1 teaspoon salt

6 quarts cold water

Wash the chicken bones under cold running water. Put the onion, carrots, celery, bay leaves, parsley, thyme, peppercorns, and salt in a large stockpot. Place the bones on top of the vegetables and cover with the cold water; the water should reach about 2 inches above the bones.

Slowly bring the stock to a simmer; it will take about 30 minutes. The bones will release fat and scum, which will float on the surface of the liquid; carefully skim it off with a ladle. Simmer the chicken stock for 3 to 4 hours, continuing to skim off any fat or scum.

Strain the finished chicken stock through a fine-mesh sieve or colander. If you are using the stock for a clear bouillon or consommé, line the colander with cheesecloth before straining to filter any impurities from the stock.

[Stock Terminology]

Stock: Produced by simmering bones, trimmings, and/or vegetables to extract their flavor, color, and nutritional value, stocks are used in sauces, soups, and stews and as a cooking liquid for braises, vegetables, and grains.

Demi-glace: A thick, velvety sauce made from a stock that is cooked for 8 to 10 hours over low heat to reduce it by as much as 90 percent.

Jus: The natural meat juices that collect in the pan during cooking, or a broth created by browning meat, bones, and mirepoix (see opposite) and simmering with stock.

Broth: Broth is intended to be eaten on its own, unlike stock, which is used in other dishes. Its primary ingredient is usually meat rather than bones.

Consommé: Consommés are richly flavored and extremely clear. Made from stock or broth that is cooked and clarified with finely diced mirepoix (see opposite), ground meat, egg whites, and tomatoes or lemon juice.

Court bouillon: A light and fresh vegetable stock used for poaching and steaming meats, fish, or vegetables.

Nage: A court bouillon used to cook fish or shellfish, which is then also used as a broth, containing the cooking vegetables, in which the fish or shellfish is served.

Mirepoix: A combination of aromatic vegetables—traditionally 50 percent onions, 25 percent carrots, and 25 percent celery—used to flavor recipes. A white mirepoix uses leeks and parsnips in place of some of the onion and carrots. A Cajun mirepoix uses onion, celery, and bell pepper.

To make a mirepoix, clean and trim all the vegetables, peel the carrots and trim the celery leaves to avoid imparting any bitter flavors. Cut all the ingredients the same size. For fish dishes that cook only a short time, the mirepoix should be finely diced. For longer-cooking beef stocks, the mirepoix should be coarsely diced.

Tomato paste or puree is often added to a mirepoix toward the end of its cooking time to impart both flavor and color. *Pincage* is the French term for cooking the tomato until it stiffens and turns a rusty brown color.

Shrimp Stock

We use shrimp stock as a base for seafood soups, sauces, and gumbos. At the restaurant, we reserve and freeze our shrimp shells all week—I do the same thing at home—then make the stock when we have a loaded freezer. The best stock is made with both the shells and the heads.

MAKES 8 CUPS

4 tablespoons olive oil

8 cups shrimp shells

1 medium yellow onion, diced small

1 carrot, peeled and diced small

1 stalk celery, diced small

2 cloves garlic, coarsely chopped

2 plum tomatoes, cored and medium diced

2 teaspoons paprika

1 teaspoon salt

1 teaspoon black peppercorns

2 bay leaves

1/2 bunch flat-leaf parsley

2 cups dry white wine

8 cups water

Preheat your oven to 425°F. Grease a large baking sheet with 2 tablespoons of the olive oil and arrange the shrimp shells on the pan in a single layer. Roast the shells until they are a reddish brown and become a little crisp, 15 to 20 minutes. Remove from the oven and set aside.

Add the remaining 2 tablespoons olive oil to a stockpot over medium-high heat. Add the onion, carrot, celery, garlic, and tomatoes to the pot and cook until the vegetables begin to soften, about 15 minutes. Add the roasted shrimp shells, paprika, salt, peppercorns, bay leaves, and parsley and stir to combine.

Add the white wine to the pot and cook for 5 minutes to reduce the wine and cook out the alcohol. Add the water and bring the stock to a slow boil. Adjust the heat to a simmer and cook the stock for 30 minutes. Remove the pot from the heat and allow the stock to cool at room temperature for 15 minutes before straining through a colander. Use immediately, store in the refrigerator for up to 3 days, or freeze for up to 4 months.

Fish Stock

Fish stock is the easiest and quickest stock to put together. The best fish bones to use for a stock are from small, lean whitefish, such as sole, flounder, or turbot. Avoid oily fish like tuna and salmon, as these can produce an off-flavored stock. Fish heads are also fine to use, but always remove the gills.

MAKES 6 CUPS

5 pounds fish bones, cut into 4-inch pieces

1 medium white onion, thinly sliced

1 leek, white part only, thinly sliced

2 stalks celery, thinly sliced

1 carrot, peeled and thinly sliced

2 cups white wine

8 cups cold water

3 sprigs flat-leaf parsley

1 teaspoon fresh thyme

1 teaspoon black peppercorns

1 teaspoon kosher salt

1 bay leaf

Combine all the ingredients in a large stockpot, bring to a slow boil, and immediately turn the heat down to a simmer. Gently simmer for 45 minutes, occasionally skimming any scum that rises to the surface. During the cooking, do not stir the bones, which will release impurities and can cause a cloudy stock. After 45 minutes, turn the heat off and allow the stock to sit for 30 minutes more. Strain the stock, again being careful not to break apart the bones. Use immediately, or rapidly chill the stock if you are reserving it for use later. (To make the ice bath, put the bowl of stock in a larger bowl filled with ice water.) The stock will keep in the refrigerator for 3 to 4 days.

Court Bouillon

Although this court bouillon can be used for poaching meats, fish, and vegetables, the recipe can also be adjusted to complement the item you are poaching. For Cajun shrimp and crabs, for example, we add lemons, bay leaf, and red pepper flakes, and for pork I add oranges and toasted and ground fennel seed.

MAKES 8 CUPS

10 cups water

1/2 cup white wine

1/2 cup white wine vinegar

1 large yellow onion, thinly sliced

2 carrots, thinly sliced

1 stalk celery, thinly sliced

2 bay leaves

Pinch of dried thyme

1 teaspoon black peppercorns

1 teaspoon kosher salt

Combine all the ingredients in a large pot and bring to a simmer. Cook at a low simmer for 30 minutes. Remove the pot from the heat and allow the court bouillon to cool before straining and discarding the solids. The liquid can be used immediately or stored, covered, in the refrigerator for 2 days.

Béarnaise Sauce

This rich sauce—a classic—completes a great beef tenderloin dish.

MAKES 1¹/₂ CUPS

2 tablespoons tarragon vinegar

2 tablespoons white wine

2 tablespoons finely chopped shallots

¹/₄ teaspoon freshly ground black pepper

1 tablespoon finely chopped fresh tarragon

³/₄ cup unsalted butter

4 egg yolks

1 tablespoon water

Pinch of kosher salt

Pinch of cayenne pepper

Squeeze of fresh lemon juice

Place the vinegar, white wine, shallots, pepper, and half of the tarragon in a small saucepan and bring to a simmer. Reduce the mixture by half, remove from the heat, and set aside.

Place the butter in another small saucepan and melt over medium heat until the butter lightly froths, being careful not to brown the butter solids. Remove from the heat and set aside.

Pour the shallot mixture into a food processor and add the egg yolks and water. Turn the machine on and slowly drizzle in the warm butter; it should take about 2 minutes to drizzle all of the butter into the sauce. Turn the machine off and add a pinch of salt, the cayenne, the remaining tarragon, and the lemon juice. Pulse the machine to incorporate. Keep the sauce in a bowl set in a larger bowl of warm water until ready to serve.

Creamy Horseradish Sauce

A creamed horseradish sauce is the traditional accompaniment for roast beef. I like to add a little Creole mustard and buttermilk for added heat and tartness. For a variation, I will add a big dollop of roasted garlic to the sauce for a subtle sweet garlic punch.

MAKES 1 CUP

¹/₄ cup prepared horseradish, or more to taste

¹/₂ cup sour cream

¹/₄ cup mayonnaise

1 tablespoon Creole mustard

1 tablespoon buttermilk

¹/₂ teaspoon kosher salt

Pinch of white pepper

Place the horseradish in a basket strainer, a fine-mesh sieve, or a kitchen towel and squeeze out any excess liquid (this will keep the finished sauce from being watery). In a small bowl, stir together all of the ingredients until the sauce is smooth. If you prefer your sauce hot, stir in up to another ¹/₄ cup horseradish. Use immediately, or store, covered, in the refrigerator for up to 2 weeks.

Wild Mushroom Ragout

We serve this wild mushroom ragout with grilled steaks and our wood-smoked prime rib. It uses a rich and beefy brown sauce as its base. If you haven't made a brown beef sauce to use in this recipe, you can substitute a rich beef stock and then finish the ragout with a tablespoon of blond roux. Because you will be finishing the sauce by mounting it with butter, don't reheat the sauce at too high a temperature, or the butter will separate from the sauce.

MAKES 3 CUPS

½ pound cremini mushrooms

½ pound shiitake mushrooms

3 tablespoons olive oil, or more as needed

1 shallot, finely diced

2 teaspoons chopped fresh thyme

Kosher salt and freshly ground black pepper

½ cup dry sherry or Madeira

1½ cups Brown Beef Sauce (page 243)

2 tablespoons cold unsalted butter

Clean the mushrooms with a brush or kitchen towel to remove any dirt. Cut the ends off the stems of the creminis, and remove the entire stem from the shiitakes. Quarter each of the mushrooms and place in a bowl.

Heat a large sauté pan over high heat and add the olive oil. Add the mushrooms in a single layer. Allow the mushrooms to brown on the first side, about 3 minutes, before stirring to brown on the other side. You may need to add a splash of oil to the mushrooms if the pan becomes very dry. After about 5 minutes, add the shallot to the pan and season the mushrooms with the thyme, salt, and pepper and cook for 1 minute more.

Add the sherry and deglaze the pan, scraping any of the brown fond off the bottom. Add the beef sauce and bring to a simmer. Remove from the heat and finish by stirring in the cold butter. Keep the sauce warm until ready to serve.

Border Chimichurri

Chimichurri is a fresh green sauce that is finished with oil and vinegar. It originated in Argentina and is popular in Mexico for serving with grilled and roasted meats. We serve chimichurri with beef, lamb, and game, and it's also great on a meaty piece of grilled fish, like salmon, tuna, or swordfish. The Mexican version is usually spiced up with some fresh jalapeño or serrano chiles. You can control the heat by using more or fewer chiles.

MAKES 2 CUPS

2 large shallots, finely diced

1/2 cup chopped flat-leaf parsley

1/4 cup chopped cilantro

4 green onions, white and green parts, minced

1 serrano chile, stemmed, seeded, and finely chopped

1 teaspoon sugar

1/2 cup red wine vinegar

1/2 cup olive oil

Kosher salt and freshly ground black pepper, to taste

In a bowl, stir together all of the ingredients. Use at once, or store in a covered container in the refrigerator for up to 2 days.

Ancho Mole Sauce

Lightly flavored with cinnamon, Mexican chocolate is sold in Latin markets and specialty stores.

MAKES 2 CUPS

1 tablespoon white sesame seeds

1 cup Salsa Roja (page 249)

1/2 cup chicken stock

1/3 cup (2 ounces) chopped Mexican chocolate

2 tablespoons raisins

Pinch of ground cinnamon

Pinch of freshly grated nutmeg

Salt and finely ground black pepper

In a saucepan, toast the sesame seeds over medium heat until lightly browned. Add the salsa, stock, chocolate, raisins, cinnamon, and nutmeg and bring to a simmer, cooking for about 5 minutes until the chocolate has melted. Transfer to a blender and puree until smooth. Return to the saucepan and season to taste with salt and pepper.

Fennel Salsa Verde

This is a traditional rustic Italian fennel sauce usually served with roasted and grilled meats and fish. The freshness of the fennel and the herbs combined with the sharpness of the vinegar works equally well with lightly grilled fish or a crusted slow-roasted piece of meat. Be sure to use a sharp knife, and finely dice the fennel, shallot, and parsley all to the same size.

MAKES 2 CUPS

1/2 cup finely diced fennel bulb

1/2 cup finely diced shallot

1/2 cup finely chopped flat-leaf parsley

1 tablespoon capers, chopped

1 anchovy fillet, finely minced (optional)

Juice and zest of 1/2 lemon

3/4 cup olive oil

2 tablespoons sherry vinegar

Kosher salt and finely ground black pepper

In a bowl, stir together the fennel, shallot, parsley, capers, anchovy, lemon juice and zest, olive oil, and vinegar. Taste and season with salt and pepper to taste. This salsa is best served fresh but will keep in the refrigerator for about 1 day.

Carmen's Green Salsa

I unashamedly stole this recipe from Carmen's in Marfa, Texas. I ran into one of the waiters at a local beer joint playing pool, and I wore him down until he finally gave me the recipe. If you don't have poblanos, the salsa is just as good made with green Anaheim or New Mexico chiles. The heat of the salsa will vary depending on the heat of the peppers you are using. If you want an extra kick, add a few roasted jalapeños.

MAKES 3 CUPS

4 poblano chiles, roasted, peeled, seeded, and coarsely chopped

1/2 small yellow onion, coarsely chopped

1 plum tomato, cored and coarsely chopped

2 tablespoons coarsely chopped cilantro

1 teaspoon kosher salt

1/2 teaspoon finely ground black pepper

2 tablespoons white wine vinegar

2 tablespoons water

Combine all the ingredients in a blender. Pulse 4 to 5 times until the ingredients come together into a chunky salsa. Serve at once or store in a covered bowl in the refrigerator.

Red Table Salsa

There are as many recipes for salsa as there are cooks. This is a solid recipe for a great cooked salsa that is served at a lot of Tex-Mex restaurants in Texas. I use serrano peppers in my salsa because I prefer their flavor and heat level, but feel free to use jalapeños if you like. If you're making the salsa in the blender, be careful not to overblend it. It's easy to incorporate too much air into the tomatoes, turning the salsa pink and frothy.

MAKES 3 CUPS

6 ripe plum tomatoes, cored and halved

2 serrano chiles, stemmed, seeded, and coarsely chopped

1/2 small white onion, coarsely chopped

1 large clove garlic, halved

1 teaspoon salt

2 cups water

1/4 cup coarsely chopped cilantro

Juice of 1 lime

Kosher salt and freshly ground black pepper

Combine the tomatoes, serranos, onion, garlic, and salt with the water in a saucepan. Bring to a simmer and cook until the tomatoes begin to soften, about 3 minutes.

With a slotted spoon, remove all of the vegetables from the water and transfer to a food processor or blender. Add the cilantro, lime juice, and salt and pepper. Pulse until the mixture is combined but still chunky. Chill the salsa in the refrigerator for about 1 hour before serving. If you must, you can sample a small bowl of the salsa with plenty of tortilla chips before you put it in the fridge to cool.

Rustic Chile Pepper Sauce

Be warned: This sauce is not for the faint of heart. I can eat this stuff all day long, sprinkled on my eggs in the morning, dolloped on my beans for lunch, or made into a pepper-butter and slathered on a grilled steak for dinner. To turn this pepper sauce into more of a Louisiana hot sauce, add another cup of vinegar and allow the pepper mash to mature in the refrigerator for at least 2 weeks before straining out the solids.

MAKES 3 CUPS

2 cups stemmed, seeded, and coarsely chopped cayenne or arbol chiles

½ small yellow onion, coarsely chopped

1 plum tomato, cored and coarsely chopped

2 cloves garlic, coarsely chopped

2 teaspoons salt

1 cup white vinegar

1 cup water

Combine all the ingredients in a saucepan and bring to a simmer, cooking on low for 5 minutes. Cover the pan and turn off the heat. Allow the peppers to steep in the liquid for 15 minutes. Transfer the mixture to a blender and puree until smooth. The sauce is best after it is allowed to mellow in the refrigerator for a few days and will keep for up to 4 weeks.

Salsa Roja

This thick chile sauce is used in making enchilada sauces, adobo sauces, and moles. I'll also use it to add some spice and depth to a cocktail sauce served with seafood, to add punch to a tomato soup or tomato sauce, or to round out a barbecue sauce.

MAKES 5 CUPS

8 large ancho chiles, stemmed and seeded

1 small dried chipotle chile, stemmed and seeded

4 cups chicken stock

3 plum tomatoes, cored and chopped

1 small yellow onion, diced medium

3 cloves garlic, coarsely chopped

1 tablespoon light brown sugar

1 tablespoon vegetable oil

2 teaspoons ground cumin

2 teaspoons kosher salt

1 teaspoon freshly ground black pepper

1 tablespoon cider vinegar

In a saucepan, combine all of the ingredients, except the cider vinegar, and bring to a simmer. Gently simmer for 5 minutes. Cover, remove from the heat, and let stand for 10 minutes. Working in batches, puree the sauce in a blender. Transfer to a bowl and stir in the vinegar. Use immediately or store in the refrigerator for up to 1 week.

Fruited Herb Grain Mustard

Southerners are quick to serve a mustard-based barbecue sauce with smoked pork. The flavors of a sharp mustard sauce and a fatty piece of smoked pork just work together. When we originally put our smoked and grilled pork chop on the menu, we wanted to fancy up a mustard sauce. We added whole grain mustard for taste and texture, a spicy fruit chutney for sweetness, and some herbs for freshness. In the summer, I use peach jam in place of the chutney, with a little tarragon added to the chives and parsley.

MAKES 2 CUPS

3/4 cup whole grain mustard

1/2 cup Dijon mustard

3/4 cup fruit chutney or your favorite fruit jam

1 tablespoon finely chopped chives

1 tablespoon finely chopped flat-leaf parsley

1/4 teaspoon kosher salt

1/2 teaspoon finely ground black pepper

In a small bowl, stir together all the ingredients. Use immediately or store in the refrigerator in an airtight container for up to 1 week.

Cider-Mustard Barbecue Sauce

This is my version of a Georgia-style cider-mustard barbecue sauce. The cider and mustard give this sauce a sharp bite that is great with slow-smoked pork or a barbecued or grilled chicken.

MAKES 4 CUPS

2 tablespoons olive oil

1 small yellow onion, diced small

4 cloves garlic, coarsely chopped

1/2 cup firmly packed brown sugar

1 tablespoon kosher salt

2 tablespoons finely ground black pepper

2 tablespoons chili powder

2 tablespoons paprika

1 cup cider vinegar

1/2 cup Dijon mustard

1 cup ketchup

Heat a saucepan over high heat and add the olive oil. Add the onion and garlic and sauté until the onion begins to soften and the garlic starts to develop a little color, 2 to 3 minutes. Stir in the brown sugar, salt, pepper, chili powder, and paprika to coat the onions. Pour in the vinegar and scrape the bottom of the pan to ensure that the onion and spices don't scorch. Bring to a simmer and stir in the mustard and ketchup. Turn the heat to low and cook, stirring occasionally, for 15 minutes. Transfer the mixture to a blender and puree until smooth. Store for up to 2 weeks, covered, in the refrigerator.

Texas Barbecue Sauce

A Texas barbecue sauce has chili powder, cumin, onion, a little something sweet, vinegar, and tomato. Most barbecue guys will add some of the meat drippings from the pit to their sauce to finish and round it out. When I'm making a batch of sauce at home and don't have any meat drippings, I'll start the sauce by adding some bacon fat to the butter that I use to sauté the onions. In Texas, a barbecue sauce should never touch the meat until it is out of the pit and on the table.

MAKES 4 CUPS

2 tablespoons unsalted butter

1 small yellow onion, finely diced

2 cloves garlic, minced

2 tablespoons chili powder

1 teaspoon ground cumin

1 teaspoon mustard powder

2 teaspoons kosher salt

2 teaspoons freshly ground black pepper

Pinch of cayenne pepper

1 cup water

1/2 cup cider vinegar

2 1/2 cups ketchup

1/4 cup firmly packed dark brown sugar

3 tablespoons molasses

Heat a saucepan over medium-high heat and add the butter and onion. Sauté the onion until it begins to soften, about 2 minutes, and add the garlic. Cook the onion and garlic for another 2 minutes, stirring to keep the garlic from browning.

Combine the chili powder, cumin, mustard powder, salt, black pepper, and cayenne in a small bowl. Add the spice mixture to the onion and garlic and stir to combine. Add the water, vinegar, ketchup, brown sugar, and molasses and bring the sauce to a simmer. Maintain at a low simmer for 20 minutes. If it becomes too thick, add a little water to thin it. Serve as is, or puree in a blender for a smoother sauce. Use immediately or store in the refrigerator for up to 2 weeks.

Vinegar Barbecue Sauce

Sweet and vinegary, with a bit of heat, this is my favorite sauce to serve with a smoked pork butt or barbecued chicken. The guajillo chiles give the sauce an earthy flavor, and the chipotle in adobo gives it just the right amount of smoky heat.

MAKES 3 CUPS

3 guajillo chiles, stemmed and seeded

1 canned chipotle chile in adobo sauce, stemmed

1/4 cup firmly packed dark brown sugar

1 cup water

1/2 cup honey

2 teaspoons salt

Juice of 1 lemon

1/2 cup ketchup

1 cup cider vinegar

1 cup white wine vinegar

1 cup water

Combine all the ingredients in a saucepan and bring to a slow boil. Reduce the heat and simmer slowly for 20 minutes. Transfer the mixture to a blender and puree until smooth. This sauce is best made a day ahead to allow the flavors to come together, and it will keep in the refrigerator for at least 4 weeks.

Sources

DRY GOODS

Pendery's
1407 8th Avenue
Fort Worth, TX 76104
800-533-1870
www.penderys.com
Spice blends, chile powder, dried chile peppers

El Paso Chile Company
PO Box 1761
El Paso, TX 79949
www.shopelpasochile.com
Spice blends, chile powder, dried chile peppers, salsa

Hatch Chile Express
PO Box 350
Hatch, NM 87937
www.hatch-chile.com
Fresh and frozen Hatch chiles

MexGrocer.com
877-463-9476
www.mexgrocer.com
Achiote paste, corn masa, specialty Mexican groceries

Mitsuwa Marketplace
21515 Western Avenue
Torrance, CA 90501
310-782-0335
www.mitsuwa.com
Panko flakes, Japanese groceries

Butcher & Packer
PO Box 07468
Detroit, MI 48207
800-521-3188
www.butcher-packer.com
Sausage supplies

SEAFOOD

Pure Food Fish Market
Pike Place Market
Seattle, WA 98108
800-392-3474
www.freshseafood.com
Fresh salmon, seafood, shellfish

Fruge
Branch, LA 70516
888-254-8626
www.cajuncrawfish.com
Gulf seafood, shellfish, oysters

MEATS

Littlefield Ranch
800 South Monroe
Amarillo, TX 79101
877-548-2333
www.littlefieldranch.com
USDA prime steaks

Heart Brand Beef
404 Airport Drive
Yoakum, TX 77995
www.heartbrandbeef.com
Kobe-style beef

Broken Arrow Ranch
3296 Junction Highway
Ingram, TX 78025
www.brokenarrowranch.com
Wild boar, venison, other game meats

D'Artagnan
280 Wilson Avenue
Newark, NJ 07105
800-327-8246
www.dartagnan.com
Foie gras, duck, cabrito, lamb, other meats

EQUIPMENT

Lodge Cookware
503 South Cedar Avenue
South Pittsburg, TN 37380
423-837-7181
www.lodgemfg.com
Cast iron cookware

Bridge Kitchenware
563 Eagle Rock Avenue
Roseland, NJ 07068
973-287-6163
www.bridgekitchenware.com
Home and professional cookware

Cabela's
800-237-4444
www.cabelas.com
Sausage equipment, camp cookware

About the Authors

LOUIS LAMBERT grew up in Odessa, Texas, and is a descendent of seven generations of Texas cattle ranchers. After graduating from the University of North Texas and The Culinary Institute of America, he honed his culinary skills working in big city restaurants in New York and California before returning to his home state. Today Lou blends fine-dining sophistication with big-flavor flair at Lambert's Downtown Barbecue, Jo's in Austin, plus Lambert's Steaks, Seafood, and Whiskey and Dutch's Burgers and Beer in Fort Worth. He is also a founding member and director of Foodways Texas.

JUNE NAYLOR, a sixth-generation Texan, is a food and travel writer and the coauthor of *Texas Cowboy Kitchen* and *Cooking the Cowboy Way*. June has served as a regional panelist for the James Beard Awards, is a member of Les Dames d'Escoffier, and is a founding member and director of Foodways Texas.

Index

Published in the United States by Ten Speed Press,
an imprint of the Crown Publishing Group,
a division of Random House, Inc., New York.
www.crownpublishing.com
www.tenspeed.com

Ten Speed Press and the Ten Speed Press colophon are registered
trademarks of Random House, Inc.

Library of Congress Cataloging-in-Publication Data
Lambert, Louis, 1958–
Big ranch, big city cookbook: recipes from Lambert's Texas kitchens
    / Louis Lambert and June Naylor. — 1st ed.
        p. cm.
Includes index.

Summary: "A collection of more than 125 recipes by Texas chef and
    restaurateur Lou Lambert, with an emphasis on regional special-
    ties and ingredients including game meat dishes and Tex-Mex
    favorites"— Provided by publisher.

1. Cooking, American—Southwestern style. 2. Mexican American
    cooking. 3. Cooking (Game) 4. Cooking—Texas. 5. Cookbooks.
    I. Naylor, June. II. Title.
TX715.2.S69L28 2011
641.5979—dc22
                2011004416

ISBN 978-1-58008-530-4

Printed in China

Design by Toni Tajima

10 9 8 7 6 5 4 3 2 1

First Edition